STAPLES
The Office Superstore

# STAPLES FOR SUCCESS

# STAPLES

 KNOWLEDGEXCHANGE

Santa Monica

# FOR SUCCESS

FROM BUSINESS PLAN TO
BILLION-DOLLAR BUSINESS
IN JUST A DECADE

## Thomas G. Stemberg

**Knowledge Exchange, LLC**
**1299 Ocean Avenue**
**Santa Monica, California 90401**
**In association with Wordworks, Inc.**
**Boston, Massachusetts**

Jacket and text design by Lee Fukui
Jacket background photograph by H. D. Thoreau/Westlight.

1 2 3 4 5 6 7 8 9-VA-99 98 97 96
First printing November 1996
ISBN: 1-888232-24-2

Knowledge Exchange books are available at special discounts for bulk purchases by corporations, institutions, and other organizations. For more information, please contact Knowledge Exchange, LLC, at: (310) 394-5995 (voice) or kex@kex.com (e-mail).

# CONTENTS

MILESTONES IN STAPLES' HISTORY

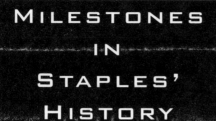

# MILESTONES IN STAPLES' HISTORY

## 1982

Ten years out of Harvard Business School, Tom Stemberg, now an executive with Star Markets in Boston, establishes himself as an innovator in the supermarket industry, and develops the first line of "generic" foods sold in America.

## 1985

**January :** When First National puts Edwards-Finast up for sale, Stemberg is fired. With a year's severance pay in his pocket, he looks for ways to give customers deep discounts on products they need every day.

**June:** An idea is born. Unable to find a printer ribbon late one Friday afternoon, Tom Stemberg asks why there isn't a supermarket for office products.

**June–August:** Stemberg does his homework: he meets with local business executives quizzing them on how much they spend on office supplies.

**October:** Todd Krasnow, a young graduate of Harvard Business School, joins the Staples team as marketing director.

**November:** After raising $4.4 million in venture capital, Stemberg and Leo Kahn found Staples as a corporate entity.

**December:** Stemberg's business plan forecasts sales of $42 million in three years.

## 1986

**December:** On a shoestring budget, the Staples team sets up offices in an old 5,000-square-foot mill on California Street in Newton, Massachusetts.

**January:** Staples officially begins administrative operations with five officers: Stemberg, Hart, Leombruno, Korian, and Krasnow.

**February:** Vendors begin visiting Staples corporate headquarters in Newton.

**March–April:** Myra Hart secures permits for refurbishing a dilapidated former auto repair facility in Brighton, Massachusetts.

## 1983

Stemberg's style catches the eye of Leo Kahn, CEO of Purity Supreme, a chief rival in the local supermarket industry. Kahn is a pioneer in the discounting of prescription drugs and an expert in high-volume sales at lower prices.

## 1984

Recruited by First National Supermarkets, Stemberg takes over as president of Edwards-Finast.

**August:** Stemberg considers a name for the new store. For the time being, he proposes the name "8 $\frac{1}{2}$ x 11." Later, he comes up with a new name: "Staples The Office Superstore."

**September:** Myra Hart, an executive at Star Markets in Boston and a fellow student at Harvard Business School; Bob Leombruno, a businessman who had helped rescue retailer Mammoth Mart from bankruptcy; Paul Korian, a merchandising executive for Osco Drug join Stemberg in pursuit of the Staples dream.

May 1, 1986—founders Tom Stemberg (left) and Leo Kahn at the grand opening of the first Staples store in Brighton, Massachusetts. Leo and Tom, who pioneered the $14 billion office superstore industry, were initially rivals in the supermarket industry before becoming cofounders of Staples.

**April:** Construction crews begin work on the Brighton store, the first Staples store in America, inauspiciously located between the Massachusetts Turnpike and the Charles River.

**April:** Staples promises to save small businesses an average of 30 to 70 percent on office supplies.

**May:** With 11,310 square feet of selling space, the first store opens in Brighton, Massachusetts, advertising Post-it Notes for $3.99 (other office products dealers were charging $11.55).

1987

**August:** An issue of *New England Business* reports that "shopping carts symbolize Stemberg's breakthrough in office supplies retailing: high-volume sales, low-margin retailing."

**September:** Pat Sher starts Office Depot, one of Staples' first competitors.

**November:** A second store opens in Woburn, Massachusetts.

**January:** Incorporated as a Delaware corporation, Staples puts up 3,737,500 shares of stock for sale at an initial offering price of $1 per share.

April 1987—Tom and Leo celebrating the grand opening of the third Staples store in Providence, Rhode Island. Little did they know that Staples would grow to be the sixth company in U.S. history to achieve $3 billion in annual sales within 10 years of start-up.

**May:** Staples' first fiscal year ends, barely including the opening sales at the first store. Staples shows an operating loss of $963,000 on sales of $8,000. At the time it has about $3 million in working capital.

**July:** Fourteen million dollars in venture capital comes from investors at Hambro International Venture Fund, Citicorp Investment Management, Security Pacific Capital Corporation, and others.

**April:** Staples opens its third store in Providence, Rhode Island.

**May:** At the end of its fiscal year, Staples announces the strategy of focusing its growth in the Northeast and establishing a centralized distribution center.

**May:** In its first full financial year, Staples reports total sales of $8.8 million, with an operating loss of $2.6 million. The company announces plans to open stores in Westchester County, New York.

**June–December:** Staples opens six new stores in Portchester and Yonkers, New York; West Springfield and Natick, Massachusetts; Springfield, New Jersey; and Carle Place, New York.

## 1988

**February:** Staples offers delivery service to its clients.

**February:** Staples opens its first store in Manhattan. For a delivery fee of $4 a box, Staples promises to bring products directly to customers' offices.

**April:** At a cost of over $6 million, Staples opens its first distribution center in Putnam, Connecticut, where the company plans to house $10 million in inventory.

February 1988—Staples brings the savings to New York. Celebrating the grand opening of the first Staples Office Superstore in Manhattan are *(left to right)* Dinny Starr, Una Finn, Demos Parneros, Suzanne Gramaglia, Alan Berkowitz, and John Hughes.

**April:** Staples adds another five stores to its lineup as well as a 30,000-square-foot consolidation center in Thompson, Connecticut.

**April:** New Jersey, Pennsylvania, and Virginia welcome Staples with the opening of 3 new stores.

**September:** Stores are now open in Philadelphia, Pennsylvania, and Silver Spring, Maryland.

**October:** Staples reports that many of its earliest stores were generating annual sales of $10 million.

**October:** Staples targets California, primarily the Los Angeles area, as its new growth hub for the 1990s. Its chief rivals are Office Club (with 10 stores) and HQ Office Supplies (with 14 stores).

**April:** At the end of its fiscal year, Staples announces that increased sales outpaced net losses for the first time achieving the milestone goal of becoming a profitable company. Sales for the year totaled about $120 million, with net losses for the entire year of $1.9 million.

**April:** Staples goes public. Over two million shares of common stock were sold through an initial public offering (IPO). Proceeds of approximately $36 million were obtained, net of offering costs. Shares initially were thought to be offered at $13, but keen interest bumped the opening price to $19. The stock soared to as high as $36 in the course of the next two years before settling down in 1991.

**April:** More than 240,000 businesses and organizations are purchasing office supplies from Staples.

**May:** Montgomery Securities reports that "Staples is in excellent financial condition" after its IPO "raised over $36 million." After building another 16 stores, Staples would still have over $18 million from the sale, enough to finance its store expansion in FY89.

**May:** Staples reports sales of roughly $40 million (an almost 500 percent increase from the previous FY) and an operating loss of $8.5 million in FY87. A total of 16 stores opened, and the company was "on a roll."

**June:** Staples' superstores on average had about 16,000 square feet of selling space carrying roughly 5,000 stock-keeping units (SKUs).

**July:** The first Staples store opens in Connecticut in Stratford.

## 1989

**January 18:** The inauguration staff, preparing for the upcoming ceremonies to install George Bush as president, order 240 plastic file cases from the Tyson's Corner branch of Staples at a total cost of $1,288.

**February:** Staples introduces its private-label products.

**April:** After a tentative start, Staples initiates "Staples Direct," a direct-delivery catalogue for business. A central call-in facility is established in Newton, Massachusetts.

**July:** Sales per square foot in Staples stores reach $480.

**September:** Outlook for 1990 has Staples expanding from 38 stores to more than 70, expected primarily in Boston, New York, Philadelphia, and Washington, D.C.

## 1990

**February:** The *New York Times* predicts a shakeout in the crowded field of office supply retailers. The stock price of United Stationers, Inc., a formidable competitor, fell by 50 percent in a little over seven months.

**April:** Staples opens its first store in Europe in Hamburg, Germany.

**June:** Staples pursues its continuous development of employees and fosters "pride of ownership" at every level of the company with programs such as Employee Stock Ownership Plan ESOP, Employee Stock Purchase Plan (ESPP), management training programs, and programs to develop customer service skills and product knowledge.

**November:** Staples opens its second store in Germany.

**December:** Staples signs a definitive agreement to acquire lease rights and certain other assets of 10 Los Angeles store locations from HQ Office Supplies Warehouse for $16.7 million.

**May:** A 130,000-square-foot distribution center opens in Fontana, California.

**June:** Staples stores now include an extensive business machine section with specially trained associates available to assist with buying decisions.

**June 25:** Staples shareholders approve an amendment to the company's Certificate of Incorporation to increase the authorized number of shares of common stock from 20 million to 40 million. The board of directors also approved a three-for-two stock split of the company's common stock effected in the form of a 50-percent stock dividend.

**June:** Staples completes a $75 million convertible debenture financing, providing the company with additional capital for growth.

**July:** The Kentucky-based store opens.

**July 9:** Staples opens store 50 in Anaheim, California.

**August:** Staples opens its first prototype Staples Express unit on Court Street in the heart of Boston's downtown financial district.

## 1991

**December:** Staples is named 1990 "Retailer of the Year" by the Office Products Show Daily Newspaper.

**December:** Staples moves its products packaged in very large boxes to a new 100,000-square-foot distribution center in Plainfield, Connecticut.

**January:** Staples reports a 64 percent increase in sales for FY90 over those for the previous fiscal year.

Staples formula was simple: Cut the cost of office supplies in half.

**July:** Dividend is distributed to shareholders on record as of June 26, 1991.

**October:** A public offering of 2,990,000 shares of common stock at $23 per share raised approximately $65 million, net of costs associated with the offering.

**October:** Staples embarks on a joint venture in Canada with Canadian superstore chain Business Depot. Staples purchases a 16 percent stake for about $2 million in the upstart venture as it opened two stores each in Toronto and Missassauga, Ontario.

1992

**October:** Canada gets its first Staples superstore in Concord, Ontario.

**December:** At year's end, Staples' stores number 123 with locations throughout the United States, in Canada, and in Germany.

**January:** The company now boasts more than 5,000 employees.

**June:** Staples acquired 10 WORKplace stores in central Florida from Office Mart Holdings Corporation in a pooling-of-interests merger.

**August:** Staples successfully converts its 1990 7-percent convertible subordinated debentures, worth $75 million.

**August:** Staples acquired a 48 percent interest in MAXI-Papier, operator of eleven superstores in Germany.

**December:** Staples buys an equity interest in Eastman Corporation, one of the leading contract stationers.

**December:** By the end of 1992, nearly 60 more locations had opened their doors, including the first stores jointly owned by Staples and Business Depot in Toronto and Missassauga.

**March:** Founder Tom Stemberg points to several key achievements that contributed to the firm's ongoing success: sales and profits of Staples Direct, the delivery service to large customers; the sales and store growth of Business Depot, the Canadian office superstore chain in which Staples then owned a 20-percent interest; successful conversion of the 1990 7-percent convertible subordinated debentures ($75M) in August; being the market share leader in all their major markets; and being the low-cost provider of office products and services to targeted customers.

**June:** Staples Express stores continue to thrive, offering seven to eight thousand square feet of space and stocking roughly 3,800 items.

**February:** For FY91, Staples reports a whopping 83 percent growth to $547.1 million, with net earnings increased 76 percent to $9.1 million. FY91 ended with 123 stores featuring more than 1.7 million square feet of selling space in total—120 of the stores were in suburban units. Earnings from the last quarter showed an astounding seventeenfold increase.

**May:** The Boston Globe ranks Staples, Inc. first on its list of the 50 top businesses in Massachusetts based on sales and profit growth.

**October:** Staples completes a new $115-million, 5-percent subordinated debenture offering.

**November:** Staples forges alliance with U.K.-based Kingfisher PLC, one of the U.K.'s leading diversified retailers.

## 1993

**January:** Staples reports that in FY92, sales grew by 44 percent to 883.1 million (despite the fact that 1992 contained one less week than the prior calendar year.) Net income for the year soared to $16.1 million compared with $9.1 million for 1991.

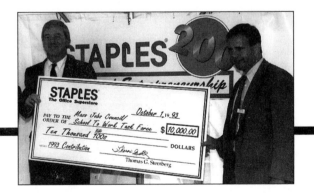

**September:** Tom Stemberg announces future plans for the opening of 345 more stores over the next five years. With this plan, Staples projected sales of about $4.16 billion by 1998.

October 1993—Staples opens its 200th store in Newton, Massachusetts. Governor Bill Weld *(left)* congratulates Tom Stemberg. By Staples' 10th anniversary date (May 1, 1996), Staples will have more than 500 superstores and 25,000 associates worldwide.

**November:** Staples announces the acquisition of South Hackensack, New Jersey-based National Office Supply (NOS), one of only two national contract stationers at the time in the United States. NOS specializes in serving the *Fortune* 1000 community.

**November:** Staples announces a second acquisition: Spectrum Office Products, Inc., a regional contract stationer headquartered in Rochester, NY.

## 1994

**January:** Staples announces that it will grow by another 120 stores to a total of 350, including 90 new North American stores (plus the acquisition of Business Depot's existing 30 stores to be completed in 1994). Staples boasts 17,000 full and part-time employees.

**January-February:** Fifteen stores open throughout the U.S., Canada, and Europe.

**April:** Staples concentrates on future growth by focusing along four dimensions: enter new markets such as San Diego, California, and Vancouver, British Columbia; increase store openings in smaller markets such as Bangor, Maine, and Lansing, Michigan, enter the contract stationer business; and start its own contract stationer operation called "Staples Business Advantage (SBA)."

## 1995

**In 1994 alone, Staples sold:** about 90,000 miles of Scotch brand tapes, over 18,000 gallons of white-out fluid, nearly 38 million pencil ad stick pens, over 725 million paper clips, and a half million rulers!

**January:** Staples announces its best year ever for FY94 with more than $2 billion in sales, representing a 53-percent increase over 1993. Net income rose 105 percent to end the year at $39.9 million. Earnings per share increased 94 percent to 64 cents per share. Store and delivery operating profits—gross profit less store operating and selling expenses—grew 58 percent to $157 million or 7.9 percent of sales. At the end of FY94, Staples had more than $260 million of liquidity to fund future growth.

**December:** The number of Staples superstores totals 230, with four new stores in the Phoenix, Arizona marketplace.

**December:** The joint venture with UK's Kingfisher is so profitable that the companies aggressively began planning to open another 10 outlets in 1994. The joint venture with MAXI-Papier is also a success and a plan for five new stores in 1994 is formulated.

**January:** Staples decides to focus on five key imperatives in the year ahead: improve customer service, accelerate and diversify North American growth, increase retail sales per store, increase delivery sales per store, and aggressively reduce costs.

**December:** Staples ends the year with 350 stores in 100 markets throughout North America and had nearly 17,000 full- and part-time associates.

May 1996—On the occasion of its 10th anniversary, Staples announced the creation of a $100,000 educational scholarship fund to benefit the children of Boston firefighters and police officers. Tom Stemberg presents Boston Fire Commissioner Martin E. Pierce with the donation.

**May:** Staples announces the acquisition of Macauley's Business Resources, Inc. (MBRI), which enables Staples to broaden its nationwide and regional contract office supply business while providing an opportunity to build upon the recent retail commitment to the Michigan market.

**September:** Staples announces changes to the names of its contract operations to better reflect how they operate. NJ-based National Office Supply becomes Staples National Advantage and would continue to serve its *Fortune* 1000 clientele. The second, Staples Business Advantage, services medium- to large-size regional companies through the five contract stationer operations Staples had acquired or started over the past several years.

## 1996

**December:** By year-end, Staples had 443 stores throughout North America, and 39 in Germany and the U.K. via its international partnerships.

**March:** Staples completes its fifth stock split in five years and announces record fiscal year earnings, making it the sixth publicly traded United States company to reach $3 billion in annual sales in less than 10 years.

**May:** On the occasion of its 10th anniversary, Staples founder and CEO Tom Stemberg announces the establishment of a $100,000 educational scholarship fund to benefit children of Boston firefighters and police officers.

**July:** Store number 500 opens in Vero Beach, Florida. Staples now employs 22,000 associates worldwide.

Staples Board of Directors (1996)—(Back row, left to right) Jim Moody, Row Moriarty, Mitt Romney, and Larry Heisey. (Seated) Bob Nakasone, Leo Kahn, Tom Stemberg, Betsy Burton, and Marty Trust. (Not pictured) Paul Walsh and Dave Lubrano.

**April:** A $1,000 investment seven years ago in Staples initial public offering would now be worth $8,000.

**September:** Staples, Inc. and Office Depot announce an agreement to merge into a single company. The new company, Staples/Office Depot, will consist of more than 1,100 office superstore locations.

AP/WIDE WORLD PHOTOS

# CHAPTER 1

# THE STAPLES CONCEPT: ANATOMY OF THE BIG IDEA

Most people adore the fairy-tale version of Staples' beginnings. I was a 36-year-old Harvard Business School graduate who had recently been fired from my job as president of a First National Supermarkets division and was working on a business plan in my West Hartford, Connecticut, home in the summer of 1985. When I began to print out spreadsheets—dozens of them—my printer ribbon broke. No problem. I'd just scoot down to Plimpton's stationery store. It was a Friday, but Plimpton's was closed because it was the Fourth of July weekend. The nearest computer store? Also closed. "Okay," I thought, "I'll run up to BJ's Wholesale Club, north of Hartford." BJ's was open. But with an inventory of only one hundred office-supply items, it didn't have my ribbon. Then, wham! A vision blindsided me: What the world needed was a superstore selling nothing but office supplies at great prices.

The incident is true, but it's hardly the real story of how a revolutionary idea evolved. The peculiar alchemy that spurred me, an out-of-work executive, to create a store that would revolutionize the way people buy paper clips and tape included these unpromising ingredients: unglamorous products, unwilling customers, and skeptical suppliers. What turned those elements into a $3 billion company in a $100 billion industry? What was it about Staples that sparked a parade of well-heeled imitators across the country? How did Staples maintain its role as an industry leader?

Not every business has the potential to grow 50 percent a year. But every business owner can learn from the Staples story. The lessons aren't ones you'll find in Harvard Business School case studies. But they have been road tested by one of the most

---

**IN MY OWN WORDS**

A superstore was the answer because you had to create something with a cost structure that enabled you to keep prices low. There's a reason why nobody had low prices in office supplies. If you sold the stuff the way the old guys did it—which is to buy in small lots and try to deliver it by your own trucks and so forth—it's obvious why stationers needed high prices to support those costs. The supermarket approach, with which I was familiar, seemed like a logical way to bring efficiency into the picture. Toys "R" Us was a supermarket. Home Depot was a supermarket, basically, for bigger, bulkier goods, but essentially a supermarket. My aim was to take the same approach and satisfy customers with lower prices.

successful start-up companies in the country, contending with some of the most demanding business conditions anywhere.

The truth is that the big idea was years in the making. Like most inventions, the concept for an office-supplies super-store was the result of a number of events and personalities coming together bit by bit. I am the son of a Newark, New Jersey, restaurateur and cater-er. Within a decade of graduat-ing from Harvard Business School in 1973, I had earned a reputation as an innovator in the staid supermarket industry. At Star Markets, a Boston-based unit of Jewel Companies in Chicago, I developed and launched the first line of unbranded—or "generic"—foods sold in the country. Old hands—some of them at Jewel—predicted failure. But consumers loved it. Sales of the onetime laggard in the Boston area soared, and by 1982, Star tied Purity Supreme, a fierce local competitor, for first place.

> ## ON PUTTING THE CUSTOMER FIRST
>
> I must look at twenty business plans every week—plans from friends, peo-ple I went to school with, professors at Harvard Business School, news-paper reporters, you name it. The vast majority focus on products, ser-vices, or ideas seeking a market. This is, of course, the opposite of what we did at Staples. By focusing on the customer and filling a need we saw all around us, beginning with that one experience I had with the broken printer ribbon, we built success on the fact that we saw a market looking for a store like Staples. That's what sets us apart from the rest.

That experience laid the foundation for Staples in two important ways. First, it earned me the respect of Leo Kahn, the flinty chief executive of Purity Supreme who built his com-pany into Boston's highest-volume food retailer largely because he introduced warehouse food stores to New England. Second, it confirmed for me the power of identifying and satisfying a customer's need, a lesson that had been drummed into me at Harvard. In this case, consumers' desire for low grocery bills was especially strong, because double-digit inflation was driving food prices higher month by month.

First National Supermarkets, my next corporate home, gave me hands-on experience with another key component of Staples' future success: warehouse selling. As president of the company's loss-riddled Edwards-Finast division, I once again focused on fulfilling customers' need for low prices, but this time I changed the setting. Instead of offering a few aisles of low-priced generics, I created gigantic stores carrying Edwards-Finast brand products. The stores' rock-bottom prices were the result of the rock-bottom costs associated with buying in volume and operating a no-frills store.

If the owners of First National Supermarkets had not put the company up for sale, I might still be in the supermarket industry. Instead, during sale negotiation, First National fired me in December of 1985. I was outraged—and scared. I had a two-year-old son and a

---

## MEGATREND

John Naisbitt's *Megatrends* had just been published, and I was out of a job and looking around for opportunity . . . any opportunity so long as it could maintain my interest. Naisbitt's book spoke to the small end of the market for consumer products and services, and it was clear that the market was growing. He saw that an ever-growing number of people would be working out of their homes, operating small businesses, opening home offices, and they would all need office products. The idea behind Staples might not have been so successful twenty or thirty years ago, but now the time was right. Isn't that what they say about success: being in the right place at the right time with the right skills or products for the right people?

There's a lot of truth to that prescription, but it's not just a matter of fate. You can make these right things come together in the right way.

household to support. Would I be able to get another job in the industry with this blot on my record? Fortunately, I had advantages that softened the blow. First National paid my salary for a year, and I was able to tap the expertise of onetime competitor Leo Kahn. He had sold his supermarket chain to Supermarkets General in 1984 for $80 million and was frustrated in his search for a new business opportunity. On hearing that I had been fired, Kahn's first reaction was surprise. His second: "I had respect for him [Stemberg]. I wanted to see if we could go in together on a new venture." Together we began to search for retailing opportunities.

I was also intrigued by questions raised by Walter Salmon, a friend and Harvard Business School professor: "Why try to excel in an industry replete with up-to-date competitors? Why not start your own business, a business that brings the modern techniques of distribution used by supermarkets to a nonfood product?" posited Salmon. The questions struck a chord. My experiences at Star and Edwards-Finast had given me a taste for shaking up the status quo. In my experience, boldness worked. This appetite for novelty allowed me to look for a chance to deploy proven business strategies (low prices and warehouse selling) in a new arena. It prompted me to look outside the mainstream. And so ordinary details—hardly noticeable to most businesspeople—leapt out at me.

The defining moment came on a Saturday afternoon in January of 1985. Makro, a struggling group of warehouse-style stores owned by two European companies, had been interviewing me to become CEO of its U.S. operation. As a devoted fan of Harvard's basketball team, I decided to tour one of Makro's stores in Langhorne, Pennsylvania—after attending a game in nearby Princeton. With Harvard victorious for the first time in 25 years, I was exhilarated as I entered the store. Within minutes, however, I knew the store wouldn't work in the U.S. It was gigantic and the prices were good. But the store concept was a mess. Instead of focusing on a single type of product, Makro had everything: apparel, food, electronics, even toys. Nevertheless, one detail caught my eye: Makro's office supplies were flying off the shelves. That was the day the idea formed: Could we create a Toys "R" Us for office supplies?

### REAL-LIFE LESSON

*Groundbreaking business ideas don't spring full-blown into entrepreneurs' brains.*

It's a myth perpetuated in magazines and books, and even by other entrepreneurs. In hindsight, a business' creation looks preordained. But in fact, the most creative ideas spring from long and intense experience with the components of the yet-to-be-created business. If I had not mastered the fundamentals—low pricing and warehouse-style selling—I would have never spotted the chance to use those selling techniques in office supplies.

## Low Prices: A Solution to a Problem Nobody Has?

I was gratified by Kahn's enthusiasm for the office supplies superstore concept. Bob Nakasone, president of Toys "R" Us and a friend from my Jewel days, was also gung ho. But I wasn't satisfied until I had exhaustively researched the idea.

I started by simply interviewing every small-business owner I knew: my typist, my dry cleaner, my lawyer, my doctor, and so on. "What do you spend on office supplies?" I asked. Nobody knew. They'd guess. So I pressed harder. One of my friends, Coleman Levy, a lawyer in Farmington, Connecticut, told me that his annual tab for office supplies was about $10,000, or $200 per employee. Appealing to his frugal nature, I challenged Levy to check his invoices. Together we pawed through dozens of bills. We discovered office supplies were actually costing Levy $1,000 per employee. He was spending $50,000 a year. Levy was aghast.

Once you explain to people how badly they're getting ripped off, and how much money is involved, you can actually create demand for low prices. But it is not an easy sell, because they don't realize they have a problem. They have a problem all right—they just don't know they have a problem. It was a fascinating lesson—but a puzzle. If small-business owners believed their office-supply expenses were negligible, they'd hardly be enticed by low prices.

The next question to answer: What kind of bargain would Staples be able to offer small-business owners? To figure out what buyers of copier paper, paper clips, and other office supplies were currently paying, I posed as a potential customer of Boise Cascade and other dealers. First, I called on behalf of

Ivy Satellite Network, a small company I owned that broad-casted events of Ivy League schools to alumni around the world. Boise Cascade, which had great prices, couldn't be bothered with sending a catalogue to Ivy Satellite, much less call on the tiny company.

Next, I called Boise back, this time representing the hundred-person office of Fred Alper, a food broker friend in Boston. This time Boise was happy to trot out to Alper's office, and I was astonished by what they offered. A Bic pen from Boise would cost Alper just 85 cents. At the mom-and-pop stationery store that poor Ivy Satellite was forced to use, the price was $3.68. Discounts from large dealers just weren't available to 20-person companies. The most I could ever talk a dealer into—when I told him Ivy was going to be the next ESPN—was a 20-percent discount.

Further research confirmed my discovery. Small companies were paying through the nose, while large companies could command huge discounts. An aggressive office manager for a company with a thousand or more white-collar workers could obtain discounts of up to 50 percent from dealers. But small

---

### HOW STAPLES GOT ITS NAME

While I was still thinking about work-ing for a grocery chain, Bob Reilley and I discussed the possibility of founding an office-supply store. Of course you have to have a good name, something the public can immedi-ately identify with the products and services you offer. Make it too obscure or cute, and you're doomed.

Bob and I came up with some pos-sibilities. The one that got the most attention, at first, was "8½ x 11." But that was a mouthful, so we also con-sidered "Office Mart" (but not "Office Depot"). One day while driving between Boston and Hartford, I was thinking about some catchier names— "Clips & Things," "Binders & Clips," "Pads & Pens," "Staples ..." *Staples*, The Office Superstore. It had a nice ring to it (and the play on the word *sta-ple* didn't hurt). We would provide the principal components for the office that works. I liked the sound of that.

businesses with, let's says, between ten and twenty, were lucky to get a 10-percent discount. They often paid full price.

This pricing gap was tremendously relevant information. I could visualize the impact Staples' prices would have on my future customers. "Imagine customer reaction," I wrote in my business plan during the summer of 1985, "when confronting signs like these."

### WHILE-YOU-WERE-OUT PADS
List Price $4.32
STAPLES' PRICE $1.39

### LIQUID PAPER
List Price $1.49
STAPLES' PRICE $.89

I figured I'd be able to save small companies $500 or more for each employee annually. And though they had been ignored, small companies could fuel Staples' growth indefinitely. In total, small companies buy more office products than large companies. Even 10 years ago, it was clear that small companies were in ascendancy. Out of 11 million businesses in the country in 1985, 10.8 million were small businesses. John Naisbitt's *Megatrends*, which had recently been published, predicted that the transformation of the U.S. manufacturing economy into a service economy would spawn an even greater proliferation of small businesses.

Best of all, the market for office supplies was huge—$85 billion—and already growing rapidly. Total sales of paper goods, clips, staples, and other basic supplies had grown at a 12.7-percent annual rate from 1978 to 1983, and even faster— 16.8 percent—in 1983 and 1984. Furniture and equipment, products that I saw as integral elements of future stores, had similarly fast growth rates.

The more I uncovered about the trade, the more the Staples concept looked like a slam dunk. But there was one problem that kept me up at night: Everything about my idea revolved around the allure of low prices, but low prices simply did not matter much to my target customers. In companies with 20 and 99 employees, an office or purchasing manager was in charge of ordering supplies, and these people were remarkably indifferent to how much they cost. Such employees rarely were praised for saving money because the expense was usually such a small portion of the company's revenues. On the other hand, office managers risked the wrath of everyone in the company if its stock of pens, receipt pads, or other supplies ran out. Though smaller companies, with 20 or fewer employees, were far more price conscious, they liked the convenience of having supplies delivered or shopping at a two-doors-away stationer. To succeed, I knew we couldn't just offer low prices and vast selection. We would have to change the behavior of businesses altogether.

---

### IN MY OWN WORDS:

*An Excerpt from My 1985 Business Plan*

The greatest challenge STAPLES faces is to change the behavior of office products consumers. In particular those businesses that currently have their office supplies delivered must be convinced to send someone out to pick them up. Among small white-collar businesses, which constitute STAPLES' primary market, the challenge is greatly reduced because such businesses frequently send a designated employee to visit a dealer's storefront or a mass-market channel to pick up supplies. Whatever the severity of the challenge, a primary goal of STAPLES' management will be to communicate the benefits of its new way of procuring office supplies .... Since STAPLES' ability to master this challenge will be the key to its success, management is prepared to invest heavily in marketing.

Very few who knew the industry believed it could be done. Buying supplies in stores was inconvenient, according to Ralph Margolius of Allied Office Supply in Norfolk, Virginia. In an office products trade journal, he stated, "My customers have noted that they have to devote a lot of time to shop, locate items, load and transport, and stand in long lines at the checkout counters." And Wallace Pellerin of Texan Business Products in Austin, Texas, practically wrote off customers' interest in low prices saying, "I sell product knowledge, service, . . . and I'm not going to worry about customers who want to save a dime!"

## REAL-LIFE LESSON

*The single best thing you can do to make your business succeed—at any point in time—is to focus on the customer.*

This idea has been so widely propounded that it has become trite. The key to making it a fresh exercise is to think about the customer's point of view on both an impersonal and a personal level. If I had simply come up with this idea for a product—a Toys "R" Us for office supplies—and proceeded to implement the idea, I might have failed. By researching customers' needs and behavior objectively, I discovered the huge price disparity between large and small businesses. By listening to the customers' personal points of view, I learned that many did not know they were overpaying and others did not really care. Daunting as this knowledge might have been, it forced me to realize early on that Staples' success or failure would be contingent largely on how well we could change customers' perception and behavior.

# CHAPTER 2

# ENTERING THE WORLD OF "SUBJECT TO" HIRING

While it's true that powerful ideas draw resources like magnets, it's not necessarily true that the resources show up at the right time. I faced all the catch-22s familiar to most start-ups. To attract managers to my new venture, I needed capital. To draw venture capital, I needed to demonstrate that I had an able management team. Suppliers did not want to ship products to Staples unless, of course, I could prove we could pay for them and had a store to put them in. Landlords were not interested in leasing store space to a start-up if it didn't have a strong balance sheet and the confidence of its suppliers . . . and round and round it went.

The first venture capitalist I talked to said, "I'm not going to finance this. There's no management team." So then I assembled a management team, and they said, "Do you have any money?" Everyone's participation is subject to something else. You live in a world of "subject to."

The only way to put the pieces of the puzzle together was to work on all fronts simultaneously. I started courting future employees even before I had firm commitments from venture capitalists. It quickly became clear that even with money behind Staples, I would be able to draw only on managers who fit into certain categories. I knew I would not get the smooth corporate executive who's on his way up and about to take his career to the moon. The executives who would be willing to take a flier on a start-up were either inexperienced, experienced but with limited skills, or unhappy with their employers.

> ## MALCONTENTS
>
> Starting up a business? Who's going to join you as you move from the paper of a business plan to the concrete on the sales floor? You don't get the polished executive or the star business school graduate who's out to make her mark on the corporate scene. Why would either of these people join a start-up company?
>
> What you get are the malcontents: bachelors, divorcées, and empty-nesters. We got a lot of people like this to join us as we were putting Staples together. It was a cadre of malcontents, a McHale's Navy if ever there was one.

Ian Patrick, the executive who was supposed to become Staples' very first employee, was a prime example of the difficulties I faced in hiring. From my point of view, Patrick had everything. A veteran of Xerox, he had moved on to Boise Cascade and built up its Washington, D.C., operation from a two-person sales unit generating $1 million in revenues to a $12 million business in just four years. Beyond his obvious skills as a salesman and manager, Patrick would offer Staples a vital connection to Boise, the most important vendor in the office products industry. Patrick, whose interest in joining the Staples team was strong enough that I included him in my original business plan, had a keen attraction to the Staples concept. But when it came time to actually make his move, he declined. It was hard to choose an unproven start-up over a successful career in a preeminent company.

Using a headhunter, I approached dozens of executives, painting my vision of Staples' future at 6:30 in the morning over scrambled eggs and bacon at Boston's Charles Hotel or the Atrium in Harvard Square, or over cheeseburgers at the Harvard Club. As the summer of 1985 drew to a close, it became clear that my best bets would be people who were part of the supermarket industry and had some prior connection with me—people who shared my outlook would be less likely to see Staples as a huge risk. One of them was Myra Hart, an executive at Star Markets.

## THE RIGHT WAY TO DO A BUSINESS PLAN

Ben Shapiro was one of my professors at Harvard Business School. He taught the first-year course in marketing, and one of his most often repeated lessons was this: Focus on your customer! Forget all this other nonsense that preoccupies most people when they start to write up their business plans. Forget all the advertising hype, which can catch you up in its whirlwind of bluster. The solid ground here is the customer's needs. How are you and your products or services satisfying a customer's needs? And while you're thinking about it, just *who* is your customer? So you want to sell dog food. Okay, who's the customer: The dog? The human? Or is it both?

After trying to imagine who your customer is, if you don't know, think about it some more. If you still don't know, better think about working for somebody else.

A former schoolteacher who had graduated from Harvard Business School at age 37, Hart had interviewed with me at Star and gone through the same training program that I had. Though she was a single mother with two kids in college, she had little fear about joining Staples: "Once I saw the business plan, I knew it was almost a sure winner. The idea of selling office products the way food was sold made complete sense. It was clear there wouldn't be any difficulty in making that plan come to life."

Another key hire, Bob Leombruno, also had a special appreciation for the Staples concept. Leombruno had successfully helped bring Mammoth Mart, a failed retail operation, out of bankruptcy and into the black for a group of investors. "I was convinced that it would work from day one," remembers Leombruno. Paul Korian, a gregarious 39-year-old who was running the East Coast merchandising operation of Osco Drug (a drugstore chain that is currently a division of American Stores), jumped to Staples primarily for personal reasons. Osco was in the process of moving its managers to Chicago, and Korian, a longtime Boston dweller, did not want to move. Korian filled the role intended for Ian Patrick: getting merchandise into Staples stores.

The fundamental attraction of joining Staples was the chance to get rich. Anyone turned on by the idea of overhaul-

## EVERYBODY LOVES A HARDWARE STORE

Going to Staples is like roaming around a hardware store. Both kinds of stores give us ideas on how to manage our lives and our work better. Some people just refuse to edit a memo or create a spreadsheet without a red pen or the proper pencil and eraser. Make it a mechanical pencil and sell it for a lower price than customers can get anywhere else, and you'll have people coming in to just to see what the latest gizmo is. What's more, they will probably buy it!

ing the distribution of stationery, Post-It notes, Bic pens, and other supplies to business customers was someone who saw the vast money machine that could be created by a chain of Staples stores. They would want a piece of the business, and I had no qualms about giving them one.

The pitch was this: "I'm going to give you a big chunk of stock in this thing. This is your chance. We're all going to work our tails off. We're going to work crazy hours. But here you'll be part of a retailing revolution. If you own 2 percent of the company and it gets to be worth $100 million, you're going to make $2 million." Though each member of Staples' first management team negotiated different stakes for themselves, within months of beginning the company I adjusted their shares so that each owned 250,000 shares of the 10 million outstanding—2.5 percent of the company.

My share-the-spoils philosophy wasn't pure generosity. It was pragmatic. Sharing ownership unifies self-interest with the company's best interest. Instead of asking whether a decision will hurt his chance for promotion, or her importance within the company, the ultimate measure becomes: How will this affect the company's success?

Also, I had little to offer besides stock. Venture capitalists had made it clear that they expected my team and me to take 33 percent pay cuts. (Because they are putting up the money, venture capitalists impose such financial duress to ensure that an entrepreneur and his managers will work like maniacs to make a success out of a new venture.) I had been earning $240,000 at First National Supermarkets, and I was required to cut my pay to $170,000. According to Myra Hart, "When we got our stock it was worthless. We took a cut in income and invested at least twice as much labor as we would have in our previous jobs."

I had to recover from some hiring mistakes immediately. Because Staples' success was dependent on changing the buying habits of its target audience, I knew that I had to find a marketing professional before venture capitalists would commit their funds. I hired an advertising executive at Mintz and Hoke Advertising in Avon, Connecticut, whose team had designed the advertising campaign that helped turn around my Edwards-Finast division. But the executive's expertise was in broadcast advertising. What Staples needed was someone who could pull customers into the store with specials, direct-mail campaigns, and promotions. Within a few weeks of Staples' corporate launch—Hart, Korian, Leombruno, and I were working feverish 70-hour weeks—we noticed the new marketing manager had withdrawn to his office to work on a big project. The mysterious work in progress turned out to be hand-drawn invitations to his own upcoming housewarming party. Shortly thereafter, he left the company.

I cast about for someone to fill the crucial marketing function and found Todd Krasnow, a 28-year-old Harvard Business

---

### THERE'S MORE TO STAPLES THAN POST-IT NOTES

We started out selling printer ribbons and Post-it Notes. Eventually we were able to convince the big guys that we could sell fax machines, copiers, and printers too. But we didn't stop there. We tied in whatever machines we could get our hands on such as adding machines, calculators, and typewriters. At first we couldn't get IBM, except by bootlegging, but when we were first starting out, personal computers weren't that big in the market. So we brought in other categories that made sense for the customers we were trying to serve: desk chairs, bookcases, and other sorts of office furniture.

School graduate working, once again, at Star Markets. It was a gamble. Though Krasnow was bright and had worked for Hart, he was green. Over the board's strenuous objections, I hired Krasnow. "I had spent four years bagging groceries, stocking shelves, cutting meat, dealing with customers, and managing store departments," says Krasnow. "It was a very, very solid base in retailing and so when Tom called, it was perfect for me. I wasn't walking away from anything that was particularly special."

## REAL-LIFE LESSON

*A start-up has little to offer a well-positioned, highly talented executive.*

To get experienced executives, you have to appeal to people whose background enables them to share your vision and who are unhappy with their current position. Hiring inexperienced people is a gamble, but one that may be worth taking. Krasnow, now executive vice president for sales and marketing, is still at Staples even though many of the experienced managers I originally hired are not.

Share the spoils of your company's future accomplishments. You want everybody there committed to the utmost degree to your ultimate success, and you want a total alignment of goals. Letting your colleagues have an enlightened economic interest in your mutual success is a great way to run your business.

# Getting Started: Creating Something Out of Nothing

Staples swung into operation in January of 1986 in a style befitting its no-frills theme. The corporate office was 5,000 square feet in an old mill building on California Street in Newton, Massachusetts. The space, owned by Leo Kahn, once housed the offices of Kings department stores and still contained a few pieces of office furniture dating from the 1950s. It hardly mattered to our tiny crew of five officers and two assistants. We were focused on a much more devilish issue: how to get the first Staples store opened in just four months. We would meet every morning at about 7:00 A.M. in a session that could run from thirty minutes to two hours. Then everyone would go to work. Someone would dash out for sandwiches at lunchtime, and we would eat them together in our shabby boardroom. The workday came to a close at 9:00 or 10:00 P.M., when everyone would stop by my office and chat informally about the day's progress.

> ### MYRA HART
>
> The building sat idle and had gone unrepaired and grown outdated. Everything was antiquated. We got buckets and rubber gloves and the first few days were spent washing and cleaning up. We couldn't sit down and even begin to operate until we did that. The furniture was secondhand—old steel desks and plastic chairs. It was spartan to say the least, but that was our intention. Our whole purpose was to say, "We save money, and we save money in every sense." It was a necessity, but it was also part of our image.

"That first year we all had our eyes on the goal, our heads down all the time," remembers Hart, who was in charge of getting the store location ready. "We were on a constant adrenaline rush. Everything we did was for the first time. We usually thought what we were doing was a good idea, but we weren't really sure it would work."

The pressure was enormous. Not only were we attempting to open a store in a remarkably short period of time, we were trying to meet that schedule for a monster store that no one had ever seen the likes of before. There was no template, no example to study in deciding our course of action. Another layer of difficulty: This store was only the first. According to Krasnow, "We had to be putting in place the capability to open one store after another, so you couldn't just do what was expedient. You had to think through a set of implications and decide how to build a system every step of the way."

One of the most worrisome projects fell to Leombruno, the chief financial officer. In addition to setting up the accounting system and reporting to venture capitalists about our expenditures and forecasts, he was in charge of buying and installing Staples' central and store computer systems. The technology would have a huge impact on customers' actual shopping experience as well as the company's ability to operate efficiently. The computers had to be able to track customer purchases so that we

> **In My Own Words:**
> *My Pitch to Suppliers*
>
> You know, you suppliers are hearing a lot of malarkey from the boys throughout the industry. They're complaining that you shouldn't be selling to us. The stationery wholesalers are saying you shouldn't be selling to us. I want to tell you something. There are three kinds of people in this world. There are those who make things happen. There are those who observe what happens. And then there are those who wonder what happened. We're going to make something happen here. You have a chance to get in up front. Don't be one of those who wondered what happened. When this train leaves the station and this thing gets going, if you don't tell me you're part of it right now, somebody else will. And we're going to be very loyal to those people who leave on that first train with us.

could reorder products. Hart also believed it was crucial that the store's cash registers be easy to operate so that any employee could use them, thus reducing the chance of checkout congestion. For my part, I wanted register receipts to indicate the list price of each item, as well as the much-lower Staples price—and the even-lower price for customers who became Staples "members." No system that met every requirement even existed at that point, so we spent hours debating what to forgo, finally deciding that price comparison was the most important feature. Larry Kennedy, a member of the original management information systems team, later fashioned the country's first system of cash registers that could assign three different prices to a particular store item.

> ## TURNING A GREAT IDEA INTO A PROFIT
>
> We thought we had a great idea that could work, and it came about in a really unexpected way. The day before we opened the Brighton store, we found ourselves awash in boxes and packages of all sorts. The aisles began filling up. Things were not on the shelves where they were supposed to be—all because the packaging was a mess.
>
> Grocery suppliers are a lot better at packaging than the makers of office products. The problem was that the packaging was designed for storerooms and warehouses, not for retail sellers. In those days *(continued)*

At the same time, Leombruno scoured computer outlets and dealers to find IBM hardware at a 20-percent discount while still retaining IBM's technical support. One of the accounting firms on whom he had been depending to analyze systems seemed to be billing lots of hours without reaching any decisions. He released the firm and redoubled his efforts. During one marathon work session in February, he and Larry Kennedy and their staff worked 36 hours straight to install Staples' central computer system.

As head of merchandising, Korian's enormous task was to get suppliers to ship products to our first store. It was one of the biggest hurdles we faced. What we were proposing to the Esseltes, Gillettes, and International Papers of the world was nothing less than disrupting the distribution system of an entire industry. It would have been hard enough just to get such behemoths to ship to a new and unproven company. But we were also asking them to support a store that—if it were successful—would undercut and potentially demolish some of their best customers. "Our vision was to totally mess up the existing channel of distribution, so they were going to fight us very hard," points out Krasnow.

How did we pull it off? Any way we could. Just as in every other dimension of this start-up, friends and connections helped. For instance, Bessemer Securities, one of our investors, owned Ampad, a manufacturer of paper pads. And even though we represented a threat to the office-supply industry, I made it a point to join the National Office Products Association. Though many in the industry would come to hate Staples—Krasnow recalls being spit on by stationers in the same elevator with him at a Chicago trade conference in 1987—the trade group itself could not treat one of its own members as an enemy.

packagers would check off on the outside of the box what color items, say, file folders, were in the carton. The check would be in the middle of four boxes, and you wouldn't have any idea what color the file folders were. Bad packaging plays havoc with your inventory. Trying to track green file folders and red markers was like trying to wrestle an octopus.

Vendors, of course, are doing you a favor when they sell to you. But that day we were setting up the store, I said to myself that customers would go for a clearer system of packaging, one that would help us track inventory while it spelled out for customers exactly what they were getting.

Korian and I wooed and cajoled to get suppliers onboard. But what proved most effective in signing up most of them was our portrayal of the Staples' vision and the powerhouse it would eventually become. At one now-legendary meeting at an International House of Pancakes where Korian had assembled dozens of small and large suppliers, I spoke about Staples' substantial backing and how the store would be different from wholesale clubs, which at the time were scaring everyone associated with retailing. Staples would be big. Staples would succeed. The punch line was that if suppliers did not work with us now, they'd be sorry. "I'm going to be very loyal to those who stick their necks out for us. But it's going to cost you a lot more to get in later," I told them.

## REAL-LIFE LESSON

### *Live reality, dream the dream.*

My band of shirtsleeve managers and I had a daily diet of cognitive dissonance. The reality was that suppliers were digging in their heels, raising the specter of a store with empty shelves. The dream was that this store would not only be the first of many, but that Staples would grow big and profitable enough to become a public company—and make all of them wealthy. Instead of being a handicap, this disparity between reality and vision was necessary to get the company going—and has continued to be a vital part of Staples' ethos.

# When Nobody Shows Up: The First Store

We landed our first lease in Brighton, Massachusetts, but it was no coup. The site, with the Charles River on one side and the Massachusetts Turnpike on the other, was within sight of Boston housing projects and had failed in a number of different retail incarnations. But we were pinning our hopes on two key features: The location was easily accessible and it happened to sit smack in the middle of a high concentration of small businesses.

Myra Hart, however, had the unenviable task of turning the location into a proper store. The building had been added onto over a period of years and looked like an auto junkyard. The construction crew regularly unearthed old bumpers and wheels. But the most nerve-racking chore was getting the store's occupancy permit. Boston had a labyrinthine process for obtaining permits from the Building Department that was further complicated by our unfamiliarity with local procedures. Hart patiently shepherded our store plans through each of the five or six jurisdictions that had to approve them, responding to

---

### AMAZING THE CUSTOMER

After we opened the Brighton store, the next defining moment was the reaction we got from customers. They were wowed by the prices. They were used to paying $70 for something that we were selling for $20. It was truly amazing. Face it, there's not much romance in paper clips or staplers. The amazing fact is that people loved looking at this stuff—even the paper clips, especially when they came in five colors.

objections and resubmitting changes. It was dreary work that lasted for weeks.

Finally, one Friday in April, she got everything signed off and walked into a final bureaucrat's office to get the cer-tificate of occupancy that was required for us to obtain insurance coverage. It was 4:00 in the afternoon and the city employee refused to give her the certificate. Worse, he said he was going on vacation the following week. "I was a little naive," says Hart now. "We didn't know about all the graft going on in the department." So instead of greasing the wheels, Hart yelled. Fortunately, after spending so many days hang-ing around, she had become familiar to many Building Department employees. One of them came over to ask what was wrong and intervened on her behalf. She got our first occupancy permit.

---

**IN MY OWN WORDS**

When you hit adversities, you've got to behave very rationally and deal with all the facts at hand. But in terms of the way you conduct yourself and the way you lead others, you've got to continue to dream the dream. You can't make it fiction. You can't make it full of falsehoods, because then you'll fail for sure. But you've got to see opportunity in the teeth of adversity, and you have to seize on an opportu-nity and make it clear and paint it vividly for those around you to help them get over the challenges.

---

While Hart was perfecting the store's exterior, Krasnow and I were wrestling with the central risk of the entire Staples concept: how to get customers to change their behavior. Re-search showed that low prices were not going to attract small businesses. "There was tremendous resistance," explains Krasnow. "People said, 'Why in the world would I go to a stationery store to buy this stuff?' Because their preconceived image involved going into a 2,000-square-foot, unpleasant, dirty store that didn't have a lot of products and that had high prices. On top of that, they all said, 'I have salespeople call on me. They send me tickets to ball games. They send me flowers.' They liked that part of their job, and we were asking them to trade that for becoming a gopher!"

Despite such resistance, we opened our first Staples store on May 1, 1986. The opening day, to which everybody that anyone at Staples knew had been invited, was a great success. On the second day, we had only 16 customers, and on the third day, about the same number. Krasnow decided to bribe customers to get them in. Advertising wouldn't work.

### TODD KRASNOW

I lived a quarter of a mile from the office, it just so happened, and we worked from 6:00 in the morning until midnight. You could literally be there 24 hours a day, there was just so much to do.

There was no store like this in existence, so there was nothing with which to compare it. There was no example of how to display the product. Everything was in plain kraft paper or in boxes marked "Stockkeeping unit 7332, five hundred #10 envelopes, Gum/Win." You can't sell that. So it was a real challenge to figure out how to sell these products. We spent a huge amount of time trying to figure it out. At first we didn't display the products, so every customer would have to open every box to find what they wanted. You'd end up with all these ripped boxes all over the place, which people then wouldn't buy.

It was expensive in the Boston market, especially with our limited budget. So Krasnow paid 25 small-business managers $20 each to shop in the store and tell him what they thought. "A week later we called them back. They had all taken the money, but none of them came to the store. I was apoplectic," remembers Krasnow. Nine finally came in and gave Staples rave reviews.

That was the beginning of Staples' inventive marketing style. Krasnow continued to send out direct-mail solicitations using information from publicly available databases. He'd "bribe" customers by mail, offering $20-off coupons or free copy paper. But instead of being content to get customers in the door, he devised a plan for refining his promotions. Once they came to the store to use the coupons, we asked them to become Staples "members" by filling out a card that would include vital statistics about their companies. Now we could measure if we were getting a good return on our promotional efforts. "We might have concluded that for one-person offices, it isn't worth it to spend $20 to get them in the store," explains Krasnow. "On the other hand, for a 15-person office, it might be worth spending $100." At the time, such database marketing was almost unheard of in retailing. Now, it's commonplace.

## INSPIRATION... ONE STEP AT A TIME

I can't say that the *whole* concept of Staples came to me like a lightning bolt out of the deep blue sky. True, I did get frustrated that late afternoon when I was searching for a ribbon to fit my printer and could find no stores open. But then most successful ideas, I suspect, come in bits and pieces.

For example, once we got up and running, we realized that we needed to have some add-ons. The home-office department could be larger. And there was plenty to attract customers, old and young, into the store to look at our back-to-school lines. Plus, there were seasonal demands for seasonal products such as graduation gifts, year-end reports, and academic calendars. It was certainly what I would call another defining point in the Staples time line.

## REAL-LIFE LESSON

*If standard marketing formulas don't work, invent your own.*

There were no role models for our first store, so naturally there was no blueprint for how to reach customers. The key to Krasnow's solution was not only that he tried something different, but that he measured the results. His program would not have worked in a grocery store, because each customer doesn't spend enough to justify the cost of maintaining a database. But an office manager, on the other hand, might shell out hundreds of dollars during each visit.

# CHAPTER 3

# RAISING MONEY:
# ANGELS AND MERE MORTALS

When Bob Reilly, a partner at the Boston-based investment bank Downer & Co., sat down to chat with me one spring day in 1985, he was taken aback. He had agreed to meet with me as a favor to a friend. Face it, I was young and had a solid résumé, but I spoke in such a rapid murmur that Reilly could barely decipher a word I was saying. Though I later learned how to communicate in front of live audiences and television cameras, at this meeting I spoke in a "telegraphic mumble," as Reilly laughingly recalls.

It was an inauspicious beginning for a relationship that would prove critical to my capital-raising efforts. In hindsight, our encounter looks like simple good luck. But it wasn't. I was simply choosing the best resources for solving Staples' problems.

Reilly would become the money hub for Staples. When we first met, I was still intent on buying a supermarket chain. Downer, which specialized in U.S. acquisitions for European companies, scouted around for supermarkets and quickly discovered that the available chains were either too big or too expensive. It didn't matter, though, because I had been overtaken by the idea for an office-supplies superstore.

But I had a money quandary. Not the one most entrepreneurs confront—which is how to get capital. My difficulty was how to get capital from the right places. Leo Kahn and Danny Coven, my financial advisor, told me that they were willing to finance the whole company. Most entrepreneurs would have jumped at the offer. But Kahn was in his late 60s and Coven had just undergone triple-bypass surgery. I wanted backers who would be tied to Staples for the long haul. Equally important, I knew that his would be a capital-intensive business. I would probably need to return to my investors many

---

### ON WORKING AGAINST AND WITH LEO KAHN

In the '70s, I knew Leo Kahn only by his reputation as a fierce competitor. In one TV spot I saw, the actor playing Leo held up a huge piece of sirloin—like something they might show you at cooking school. It was a promo for Heartland Food Stores, and "Leo" had this butcher chop off about a third of the steak and throw it away. Then "Leo" looked straight into the camera and said, "At Heartland we cut the price of your grocery bill by one third."

At Star Market we responded with warehouse specials. *(continued)*

times before the company could go public. The solution, I decided, was to raise money from institutions dedicated to backing new enterprises. So I walked into Reilly's office one summer day and asked, "Do you guys do start-up financing?"

In hindsight, I have to admit that it was an ingenuous question. I knew that, as a rule, Downer didn't invest in new enterprises. But I also knew that Reilly ran a small portfolio of venture capital investments for a German family. Reilly listened as I told him about the mouthwatering business that awaited. It sounded intriguing to Reilly, so we made a deal: Reilly would help raise money for Staples, and in return, I would let Reilly's German client participate in the deal.

I started researching my scheme. Weeks went by. Finally, I dumped a big pile of paper on Reilly's desk. He plowed

that our specials had the same prices as Heartland's, but that we actually carried the item, whereas Heartland was often sold out. What good was their promise to cut prices by a third when the inventory was not there?

Kahn went ballistic. Leo said he would beat *anybody*.

In the end, we killed his campaign.

Many people in Leo's shoes at that point would say, "That bastard," and hold a grudge for the rest of their careers. Some forgive and forget. Others admire those who can compete effectively. And it goes both ways. Interestingly, it occurred to me that I might have Leo on my team sometime.

through some 200 pages of spreadsheets, written analysis, and data before he pronounced judgment: "Tom, there's some interesting stuff here—but it's not a business plan." Reilly took my materials and edited the business plan that would succeed—or fail—to persuade venture capitalists to sink millions of dollars into the Staples concept.

While the business plan was impressive, I knew it might not be enough to persuade investors to fork over cash. I stepped back, looked at my case dispassionately, and pinpointed the negatives a cautious investor might spot. Foremost among them: Tom Stemberg. While I had run a billion-dollar business—experience not many entrepreneurs could claim—I was controversial, a bit of a wild card. I had been fired. Some people from my past loved me, but others hated me. It was not the kind of profile that inspires professional investors to open their wallets. A good business plan was not going to persuade investors that my so-called wild streak was under control. I had to deal with that issue.

So I set out to make myself as acceptable as possible. My strategy: Offset the negative reviews with recommendations from people whose credibility was impeccable and surround myself with directors on whom the venture capitalists felt they could rely. Here are some of my most important sponsors and how I found them:

- WALTER SALMON: A thoughtful professor at Harvard Business School, Salmon taught me marketing and continued to offer career advice during my stints at Star Markets and First National Supermarkets. "Walter is the grand old man of retailing at Harvard, even-tempered and calming. He was important in the idea formation of Staples," says Myra Hart, who is now Salmon's colleague at Harvard Business School.

- ED CORMIER: As head of operations for Edwards Supermarkets, from which I had been fired, Cormier's recommendation was vital. Cormier's positive evaluation could not be made public—it could have damaged his career—but it was a powerful way to assuage potential backers' concerns.

- LEO KAHN: This onetime rival at grocery chain Purity Supreme became a friend after we were both guests on a local television show in 1978. Kahn had played basketball, my great passion, at Harvard. As president of a fund-raising organization called Friends of Harvard Basketball, I made it a point to include Kahn in banquets and other events. Ten years later, Kahn was looking for a new investment just when I was looking for a fresh career. "The role Leo played fulfilled many facets," says Myra Hart. "The money was important, but the credibility that Leo offered to Tom's investors was even more important." Adds Bob Reilly, "Kahn

---

### LEO KAHN'S ADVICE ON VENTURE CAPITALISTS

When Leo was younger, he was sometimes very forgetful and often got everything really screwed up. Back when we were hatching the plan for Staples, he told me to meet him at the Marriott in Newton, Massachusetts. So I go there, but there's no Leo. He's over at the Holiday Inn, waiting for me.

We finally did get together, and I learned a lot from him. Leo said he wanted me back in the business. He taught me that once you get involved with the venture capitalists, there is only one strategy that allows you to survive, only one thing the wolves really understand.

"What's that?" I asked.

"You'll get their attention if you can say—and mean it—*I don't need you*. If you do need them, they can squeeze you for a lot," Leo told me.

was tremendously successful, savvy, and a good guy. People knew that if you're in a deal with him, you know you're in with good people." Kahn also brought cash. I didn't want to completely fund Staples out of Kahn's bankroll, but it was comforting to know the money was there.

- DON PERKINS: The former chairman of Jewel Companies, Perkins has acted as a regular source of advice and counsel over the years. A director of AT&T, Time Inc. and other companies, he strongly recommended that I start my own business.

- BOB NAKASONE: Nakasone had completed the same training program at Jewel Companies that I had. By the time I began searching for a business opportunity, Nakasone was a top manager at Toys "R" Us. Smart and well versed in every detail of superstore retailing, Nakasone helped me build the conceptual framework for Staples and served as one of our first board members.

- DAVE LUBRANO: I got to know this onetime certified public accountant, who would later become a Staples director, in 1980 when we both served on the board of Superior Brands, a small pet-product maker. Lubrano was a master entrepreneur, having cofounded National Medical Care, a kidney dialysis business later sold to and spun off by W. R. Grace, and later helping establish Apollo Computer, a computer workstation company.

I discovered Reilly, the Downer partner, through my Harvard affiliation. I discussed my plans with John McArthur, a dean of Harvard Business School, with whom I had kept in touch. McArthur sent me to Chuck Sethness, an associate dean at Harvard Business School, who suggested I meet with the investment bankers at Downer. By the time Reilly and I had made our deal and were ready to search out investors, we had not only prepared the official selling document, the business plan, but also the unofficial sales force—my sponsors.

## REAL-LIFE LESSON

### *Business plans alone are not enough.*

There is no end to the reassurances that folks holding the purse strings need before they invest in your enterprise. Any question marks about it—or you—are reason enough to back off. You must foresee any major hurdles to investment before they crop up and devise a strategy to overcome them. As I started Staples, I anticipated what the questions would be and put together an infrastructure of board members, references, and managers to address those questions. The more objective you are about your greatest perceived weaknesses, the better off you will be.

## Cat and Mouse: Playing the Venture Capital Game

All I really knew about venture capitalists when Reilly and I began searching for money in August 1985 was that I needed them. I could have scared up enough money from Leo Kahn and his friend to hot-wire Staples into existence. But I knew that I had a capital-intensive business to grow. Dozens of stores would chew up many millions of dollars. The $4 million I was now seeking was a mere drop in the bucket. If I could hook a handful of venture capitalists, I would have access to gigantic pools of capital and connections to the Wall Street firms I would eventually need to take Staples public.

It didn't take long to learn that venture capitalists like to say no. In fact, we quickly learned, a venture capitalist's answer is "No, No, No"—until it's "Yes." At which point they add, "I'm going to pay you as little as possible for as much of your company as I can get." Scott Meadow, a professional investor at William Blair, summed up the venture capitalist's point of view when he replied to my pitch by saying, "Tom, what you're asking me to do is value your idea and your résumé at $4 million, and that's just high. Ask me for a million."

To be fair, it's not as easy to be a venture capitalist as most entrepreneurs imagine. While venture capitalists do control the money, they don't truly control anything else in the companies they buy into, no matter how much they own. They can't be certain that an entrepreneur's skills will fit those needed by the new enterprise, that his or her management team will work well together, or that the idea itself will fly. Even if they can exert control, such professional investors rarely have the operational savvy to force the business to succeed. They can hover in the background—or conspicuously in the foreground—but betting on new ventures is basically a crapshoot.

So it's easier to say "No" than "Yes"—and at first that's all Reilly and I heard. The Sprout Group in New York, a unit of Donaldson, Lufkin and Jenrette, heard our presentation and "politely threw us out," recalls Reilly (though they led a later round of venture financing). We got an enthusiastic hearing from one partner at Charles River Venture Partners in Boston, but the partner with veto power nixed any participation.

But there were four solid factors in our favor. I had proven myself capable of running a big company. The business plan Reilly and I had crafted stood out for its comprehensiveness and focus on customers. Leo Kahn's support gave our project a weight and authority that simply wouldn't have been pos-

> ### BOB REILLY
> *Partner at Downer & Co.*
>
> Coming out of food retailing, Tom was used to working on very thin margins—when you're buying something in that industry, you don't leave a fraction of a penny on the table. So he was driving the venture capital investors totally up the wall by negotiating every tiny point. I'd get a call from an investor who'd say, "Reilly, you've got to get over here. He's driving us crazy." My answer always was, "You're about to invest in a company with stores aimed at producing high-volume sales at low margins. Do you want a guy who is going to roll over when he's negotiating with suppliers or someone who's going to negotiate every fraction of a penny?"

sible for me to summon by myself. And most importantly, the idea for the business was so powerful, it practically jumped off the page. "Frankly, what sold us was the comparison to Toys "R" Us.

Staples looked like it could be a category killer," says Felda Hardymon, a partner at Bessemer Venture Partners in Wellsley Hills, Massachusetts, who had invited Downer to coinvest in another deal several years earlier.

But even Hardymon wasn't completely sold. He decided to invite Mitt Romney, a partner at Bain Capital, into the picture. Boston-based Bain, a unit of Bain Consulting, was a newcomer to venture capital. After running a consulting firm for eleven years, Bill Bain, its founder, became intrigued by an idea. To advise their clients, Bain's consultants regularly studied industries so closely that they could spot tremendous entrepreneurial opportunities, yet they never got to take advantage of them. Why couldn't Bain's vast analytical talent be deployed in venture capital, where there would be giant payoffs? In 1984, Romney launched Bain Capital. Hardymon thought Bain's painstaking approach would be useful in testing my research. "Due diligence was a real thing with them. You could ask a rhetorical question and some Bain consultant would go out, do research for two days, and come back with answers," he explains.

Indeed, Bain investigated every nook and cranny of the Staples premise. "At first I thought it was a crazy idea," recalls Romney. "Business services were moving toward becoming more convenient, but this idea involved asking businesses to do their own shopping." He decided to study the idea more closely. A team of four consultants called 40 companies to ask how much they spent on office supplies. Glumly, they came back with the answer: only $200 per employee. I said, "Look guys, I agree that it's not a top-of-mind problem. Do me a favor and audit the invoices." And because they were rookies, the Bain consultants actually did it. The new answer: $800 per person. The money that customers could save was, in the end, what persuaded Romney. "There were some big risks, but we knew that if people behaved as rational economic beings, they'd come shop at Staples," he says.

I then pursued Fred Adler, a New York lawyer who dabbled in venture capital, after meeting one of his junior partners, Sandy Samuels, through a headhunter friend. Samuels liked my presentation immediately. Hambro, a New York venture firm approached by Reilly, also sensed a good opportunity.

By November of 1985, Bessemer, Bain, Adler, and Hambro had finished sniffing the deal and wanted in. But in the odd world of venture capital, nobody wanted to make the first move. Explains Reilly: "Venture capitalists have a well-developed herd instinct. If one buffalo starts to run, all the buffalos will run. But if no buffalo starts, no one will run." The buffalo that moved: Adler, who was not a card-carrying member of the venture capital industry and thus had no compunction about breaking ranks with the others by saying "Yes." Bain, Bessemer, and Hambro fell into line quickly. They didn't want to lose the deal, and they hated to see Adler get it.

Negotiations, nonetheless, dragged on over price. The central tension in any venture capital deal: how much the yet-

---

**IN MY OWN WORDS**

The venture capitalists tried price fixing on me. When they said that the valuation of Staples was just too rich for them, I'd say: "I'd really like to have you as an investor. The stock is going to be sold for this price. I hope you're not upset when I don't come back to you later (in future financing rounds), because I'd like to. But I just want a fair price for the stock, and I'm going to get it."

to-be-established company is worth. A company's valuation, as it is known, governs how much money an entrepreneur raises as well as how much of the company the entrepreneur will own. Venture capitalists yearn to keep the valuation low; entrepreneurs want to push the number up. In this case, I thought Staples was worth $8 million. I wanted to raise $4 million for 50 percent of the company. The venture capitalists wanted to value the company at $6 million—which would have netted us only $2 million.

As Bessemer's Hardymon and I wrestled with the valuation issue, I grew demoralized. We knew that Staples didn't have a shot at success if it was not adequately funded. And to get the $4 million we needed, the venture capitalists were demanding between 70- and 80-percent ownership of the company. If venture capitalists were controlling the company, would we have the decision-making power necessary to make it succeed?

I poured out my concerns to Dave Lubrano over Czech beer in a Prague bar. We had flown to Eastern Europe for a Superior Brands board meeting. Lubrano, a veteran well acquainted with venture capitalists, gave me a much-needed shot of entrepreneurial boosterism. He said, "Hey, you can't trust these guys. The venture community is just out to cut the best deal they can for themselves and their partners." Lubrano emphasized how terrific the Staples idea was and encouraged me to stick to my guns. If the venture capitalists were going to be so greedy, he said, "Tell them to go screw themselves."

Thus fortified, I flew back to Boston and insisted on a better deal. Was I scared that the company would end up without backers? No. The venture capitalists operate as a cartel. I figured it out only later on. They talk to each other, and they agree on the valuation they want. I broke the cartel by getting people outside the club, like Adler, who would have been willing to invest without the others, and Bain, which was new and not really part of the club. On January 23, 1986, I struck a deal: The venture capitalists would pay $4.5 million for 56 percent of the company. Staples was worth almost $8 million.

---

### REAL-LIFE LESSON

*No one will ever value your business as highly as you do.*

That's the way it should be. No one can see a new enterprise's potential—and the steps needed to fulfill it—as clearly as the person who is risking his or her livelihood on the idea. That means you will face skepticism at every turn, particularly from potential investors. But remember: A company's valuation is as much a test of conviction as a measure of potential. No one really knows how a new business will fare.

## Round Two: Breaking the Venture Capitalist Cartel

I entered the ring swinging in round two. This time I had a lot more leverage: My idea was working in spades. We had opened one highly successful store with the first round of capital, and the prospects were bright. Sales per square foot were increasing rapidly. The first store had opened with a forecast of $4 million in annual sales, but it was quickly zooming toward $6 million a year. "We kept beating our forecasts. The results were exciting enough to cause a lot of people to sit up and take notice," recalls Bob Leombruno, who reported monthly results to the venture capitalists. But Staples would need to expand quickly. Within five months of the Brighton store's opening, a clone called Office Depot began opening stores in the Southeast. We needed more money to stake out our territory—fast.

But the venture capitalists entered round two with their gloves up, too. Now they said, "He nailed us the first round. Let's go get it back." They urged me to take a backseat in raising capital so I wouldn't be distracted from running the company. They offered to bring in a blue-ribbon panel of investors such as J. H. Whitney and Rockefeller in New York. And they had already marked up a price tag for Staples: $15 million. Venture capitalists have a rule of thumb: In second-round financing, never value a company at more than twice its first-round valuation.

I was determined to do better. Venture capitalists had pegged Home Club, a home improvement retailer similar to Home Depot, at $22 million in a recent financing. What's more, I knew that there had to be other investors willing to pay up to participate in the Staples story.

So I decided to give my venture capitalists a little competition. I asked Goldman Sachs, a New York investment firm, to prepare a capital-raising proposal. Goldman's proposal landed on my desk two weeks later. What did the firm say Staples was worth? Exactly the venture capitalists' number—$15 million. Pressing the investment bankers, I learned that Goldman thought it could raise more for Staples but had plugged in the rule-of-thumb figure after consulting with the venture capital community. Exasperated, I told them, "If you want to value the company at the same level as the venture capitalists, I don't need you. If you want to raise the amount it's worth, we can go ahead." The next day I got a call from Goldman. "Tear the valuation page out of the proposal," the bankers told me, "we've got a new one": The firm said it could value Staples at $22 million!

> **BOB LEOMBRUNO**
> *Former Chief Financial Officer*
>
> We turned money away in the first and second rounds. There was a second company called Office Depot that opened about nine months after our first round. They were run by very experienced retail people from Grossman's Lumber and functioned similarly to Staples. They were jumping all over the Southeast. Immediately all of the venture capitalists who funded retail start-ups understood the potential of these stores. You didn't have to be a rocket scientist. We were seeing sales figures of $300 to $800 per square foot. High-volume discounters were lucky to do $300 per square foot.

Armed with the Goldman proposal, I decided to call the venture capitalists' bluff. After they were all assembled around a table at the next board meeting, I told them that I had received a better offer. I told them I would be willing to cut them in on the deal at a slight discount, but that I was prepared to hire Goldman if they could not match the $22 million valuation. Bessemer dug in its heels at $15 million. Hambro waffled. Mitt Romney split ranks by saying that he didn't know what Bain Capital was willing to do, but that several of his limited partners were willing to put up their own money at my price.

The following week, while the first-round venture capitalists struggled to come to an agreement, I found two investors who had no qualms about how I valued Staples. Marty Trust, the head of Mast Industries, whose office in Woburn, Massachusetts, was across the street from Staples' second store, wanted to buy 10 percent of Staples. "Well, that will be $3 million," I said. "Fine," said Trust. Ricardo Poma, a limited partner of Bain Capital, invested $750,000, at the same valuation.

When I went back to my first-round backers, I had alarming news. It began to look like they might be crowded out. "This thing's filling up fast. Do you guys want to play or not?" I asked them. It worked. The venture capitalist group, which included Citicorp, Blair Ventures, and Security Pacific, agreed on the $22 million figure.

*The more deep pockets you locate,*
*the better your negotiating position.*

Different investors will value your business differently. Marty Trust's retailing background made him put more of a premium on Staples' high sales-per-square-foot than did the venture capitalists. I also discovered that there were plenty of other institutional investors who would be happy to accord Staples a higher valuation. Without their differing perspectives, I might have ended up with significantly less money to build the business and a smaller ownership position.

# CHAPTER 4

# OF LANDLORDS AND
# REAL ESTATE

Instant success bequeathed Staples with instant inadequacy. One successful store was not enough to make our imprint felt throughout Boston. Three Boston stores were not enough to hold off competitors from coming into the Northeast. A dozen Northeastern stores wouldn't stake out our turf across the rest of the country. Finding and securing the right real estate is a deadly serious concern for any retailer. For us it was even more so. When you're the CEO, driving around looking at real estate is the most important thing you can do. If you're in the retail business, it's everything. We couldn't afford to advertise much. Your biggest advertisement is the storefront itself. Everything rests on your ability to create a monument out there on a Route 9 or a Route 1.

The most serious roadblock to leasing stores was our short track record. The last thing a landlord wants to do is make a bet on an unproven business. What's more, any real estate owner who was interested enough to make inquiries about this revolutionary kind of store would not have been encouraged; the scuttlebutt buzzing through office-supply and stationery circles was that Staples would never make it. "When you're just starting and no one knows anything about your business, they're fearful of leasing to you and won't make any improvements to the building. The weaker your balance sheet, the higher the rent," says Steve Westerfield, former CEO of WORKplace, a competitor that Staples acquired in 1991.

Today most folks know Staples superstores as huge spaces, between 17,000 and 24,000 square feet, with red-and-white pylon signs outside. But to land a site when Staples was still a young company, we were forced into being flexible. We converted restaurants and massage parlors into Staples stores and even fashioned one California building into a flying saucer shape to satisfy Los Angeles building officials.

"Most of our jobs were frantic. In many places we ran into asbestos. We had contractors abandon jobs. One of our contractors in Portchester, New York, was literally working day and night. I'll never forget going to the store and finding his bed—he was living there until the job was done," remembers Myra Hart. Ron Sargent, vice president of operations in 1989, remembers one of the company's real estate representatives describing her tour of a prospective Staples store: "She was walking through the building and happened to look down. I guess there was some sort of toxic waste on the floor and her shoes were starting to melt."

Flexibility also meant learning how to live with even the most idiosyncratic landlords. Joe Vassalluzzo, executive vice president of global growth and development, had followed the fortunes of one eccentric Delaware landlord-developer for years. The developer owned a former elementary school in Wilmington that he planned to turn into a shopping center. But there were a myriad of environmental and zoning hurdles to clear before he could begin construction. The obstacles were so daunting that many observers believed he'd never get the necessary approvals. But the developer steadfastly held onto the property, and finally, after a decade of ownership, he was able to construct a shopping center.

Vassalluzzo began to negotiate for a site, but the potential transaction seemed doomed. The landlord wanted an outrageously high rent—some 30 percent higher than the going rate—but the location was exceptional. He also insisted that Staples conform to his center's color scheme: brick with green signage and trim. "Even though we were anxious to secure the site, we told him the rent was highway robbery," recalls Vassalluzzo. The landlord retorted that he'd find a competitor, but Vassalluzzo and his team thought it was a bluff. Nothing happened for several months. Then, out of the blue, the developer called Vassalluzzo and began talking to him in a whisper. Vassalluzzo could barely hear him, so he asked the developer why he was whispering.

"Because I'm at the other guy's place," the developer answered in a barely audible voice. It turned out that Intelligent Electronics, a Wilmington company, was contemplating opening a superstore and was interested in the site. But the developer preferred Staples as a tenant and was calling to give us one last chance to take the site. Knowing the landlord's eccentricities, Vassalluzzo believed him and decided that he was willing to pay the outrageous rent if the landlord would sign Staples' standard lease. "I'll sign anything," the landlord promised, "as long as the rent is right."

One of our Midwestern stores was built in the parking lot of a furniture store owned by a local couple. Though the couple clearly enjoyed getting a rent check from us every month, they weren't especially pleased about all of the characteristics that went along with a retail superstore. Armed with binoculars, they watched the parking lot like hawks for misdemeanors—abandoned shopping carts, employees parking in the wrong spots, sloppy trash collectors, and the like—and called promptly to complain. "You name it, it was

## JOE VASSALLUZZO

Most real estate developers who lease to us are local. In 25 to 30 percent of the cases, the property we're negotiating over is the only one they own. They're a very eclectic group, but there's a common theme. They're self-made—very driven, very assertive, and very aggressive. They're going to be adversarial. Their sense of loyalty is distorted from the usual sense of the word. I'll never forget shaking hands with a national developer at a conference I was attending. He was telling me how much he loved Staples and what a great company it is. We're standing at his company's booth, and I look up to see we're shaking hands underneath a gigantic blown-up photograph of an Office Depot store he owned—our main competitor.

an issue," recalls Vassalluzzo. "Our general manager was pulling his hair out."

Periodically the couple would become so agitated that they would summon Vassalluzzo and Sargent to a summit meeting. During one visit, Vassalluzzo walked through the large, empty furniture store searching for the couple. "It was full of totally bizarre furniture. I was getting the sensation of being on the set of *Sunset Boulevard*. In came the woman looking like Gloria Swanson, with a five-foot beehive, black toreador slacks, and heels," remembers Vassalluzzo.

The tirade began. She knew all of the Staples' employees by name and itemized their sins. One had thrown a wrapper on the ground in the parking lot during his lunch break. Another had parked in a space reserved for the furniture store's nonexistent customers. Finally, admonished the woman, "That one girl, Debby, somebody should tell her that she wears her bra too loose." Vassalluzzo looked at Sargent. Sargent looked at Vassalluzzo. "It was like the *Twilight Zone*," says Sargent.

Why bother with such eccentrics? We needed the site, of course. But we also operate according to a credo that would serve any business: Your landlord is your business partner. Recognize that a landlord is making a huge investment in you. If you sign a lease for 20,000 square feet at $20 a square foot, that's $400,000 a year. If you sign a ten-year lease, that's a $4 million commitment that guy made to you. He's betting that you're going to stay in business. If you go broke, it's going to take him two or three years to get his real estate back through the court system.

# The Agony and the Ecstasy

Our hunger for real estate grew intense in 1989. Between 1986, when Staples was founded, and 1989, we opened 25 stores. But in 1989, the competition was multiplying. Having gone public, we finally had the capital to expand massively. And we did. From 1989 to 1995, we opened a new store every eight days—nearly one a week. To pull off this astonishing feat, we had to pour resources into acquiring stores. The first step was hiring Vassalluzzo, president of American Stores Properties Inc., a subsidiary of American Stores Co. Vassalluzzo's mission: to build a real estate machine that could support

Staples' hypergrowth. Our real estate staff grew from one manager and one researcher to nearly fifteen executives who would comb the country searching for location, location, location. More important, the real estate unit developed a sophisticated software model to analyze store sites. "Today, if you give me an intersection, we can tell you the population count, small business count, and prospective store volume," says Henry Flieck, vice president of real estate.

But one key factor drove our real estate quest: boundless energy in the face of uncertainty and endless obstacles. It is not hard to find a good store location. They are there to be seen and inspected. Good research can readily show whether the place has a high density of small businesses nearby. The hard part is negotiating for a store, which can take from three months to a year. "You never have control during that time period," explains Vassalluzzo. "Yet you're planning the store and acting like you have control. Then after ten months of negotiation when you're finally set for a signature, out of nowhere a competitor comes in and says, 'I'll pay whatever to take that lease away.' You live in a constant state of fear and terror."

The "what ifs" add immensely to the uncertainty. A typical contract lease will consist of a firm ten-year commitment and a series of renewals, which usually adds twenty more years. The time span alone opens a multitude of possibilities: What if the state puts in a superhighway in the year 2010? What if all the other stores in the mall close? Who is responsible for the myriad ways the store can be damaged? Like any retail operation, we have to make extensive promises about how often our stores will be open and how long they will be open.

There is plenty to argue over. So reaching an agreement with a landlord not only takes time, it takes thick skin. According to Vassalluzzo, "The best way to describe the approach of most landlord-developers is that when you first make contact, they immediately hit you over the head with a two-by-four as hard as they can. If you survive the blow, you're worthy of negotiating with them."

In California, however, landlords use a different but equally painful approach. "They kind of befriend you. Instead of using a two-by-four, they use a 'one-by-three' and hit you softly about a thousand times," Vassalluzzo says. The best example was Robert, a Los Angeles developer who drove a Jaguar with a license plate that read "DCLAWED." Robert had remarried for the third time, he explained to Vassalluzzo, and finding the true love of his life had removed his claws. But it seemed he had also lost his ability to make quick decisions. Guided by his accountant and a financial advisor who was also his spiritual advisor, it took six months before he could even decide to begin negotiating with Staples. "I guess he was trying to become one with the universe," says Vassalluzzo. Finally, after two years of negotiation, they were able to conclude the transaction.

> **RON SARGENT**
> *President, Staples Contract and Commercial*
>
> Today there's a lot of quantitative modeling about where to place a store, but in the beginning we did things differently. We located stores in areas that were high density for businesses but were not historically good retail locations. Now we look for the density of business but also for good retail locations because a good chunk of our customers are consumers. Early on, we wanted stores to be a ten-minute drive away, but now that we've recognized that small towns are good markets for us, some stores are an hour-long *(continued)*

Hard, cold cash holds sway even in the most orderly of settings. At one bankruptcy auction, Vassalluzzo had his eye on a Framingham, Massachusetts, location in which he felt few retailers would be interested. Bankruptcy auctions, which are legal proceedings, many times turn into circus sideshows. The representatives, or agents, hired by the court are expert at generating the maximum amount of money for the bankrupt estate and have little interest in anything else. At one particular auction, a former toy superstore was available for the apparent bargain price of $350,000, with little or no prior interest in the location from other retailers. Much to Vassalluzzo's and everyone else's surprise, a bevy of retailers showed up at the court, and serious bidding commenced among the group. It was fast and furious, and the asking price quickly escalated into the $1.5 million range, to the delight of the court and the representatives. Near the bidding's conclusion, the trustee summarized the bids with the obvious intent of keeping his eye on the money and not much on anything else. As he attempted to summarize who bid what, new retailing names emerged. MVP Sports became "the sporting goods outfit." Computer City became "the computer guys from Dallas." And Fretters, a consumer electronics retailer, became "Fritters." He may have had difficulty with their names but not the amounts they bid.

> drive. I remember having this conversation with Tom about putting a store in Dayton, Ohio. Staples was in Columbus and Cincinnati, and Dayton was right in the middle. But Dayton was a big-company town with a few hundred thousand people and Tom's conclusion was: It's too small to support a superstore. Now there are four superstores in Dayton—all of them doing very well—but unfortunately none of them is a Staples store.

*In retail real estate, you spend your life trying to control things over which you have no control.*

The only way to deal with the uncertainty is to forge ahead, building your company's plans around the belief that the store will actually open while pursuing alternative sites. In August of 1995, for example, Staples' marketing, merchandising, and information systems departments were designing their operational plans on the assumption that we would open more than 100 stores in 1996, though only 35 percent of the leases had been executed. Vassalluzzo concludes, "A deal is not a deal until it is signed, no matter how many conditional letters of contract you've signed, no matter how many hands you've shaken."

## Stealing Home Base: Defensive Real Estate

The beauty of nailing down a prime store location is that in one fell swoop you establish your presence while preempting that of your competitors. Because the market for office-supplies superstores is far from saturated, securing real estate continues to be as much a key competitive strategy as it is a fuel for growth. "It's a race," explains Vassalluzzo. "Real estate is like diamonds—scarce and irreplaceable. Once you have it, the chance of a competitor finding something comparable is slim. There's an ending to the story. Eventually there will be a saturation point. The total number of superstores that North America will support? Probably 2,800 retail stores or more. By the end of this year there will be about 1,400 stores."

Prime properties stimulate as much intrigue as a Tom Clancy best-seller. Scuttlebutt about store sites circulates constantly among brokers, agents, store representatives, and merchants. It is no secret that a choice spot will be coming on the market. The secret is how to get it—or keep it away from your competitors. In one of our biggest victories in the turf war, we had been trying to snare three Baltimore stores that had belonged to Office Stop, a competitor that had gone bankrupt. The bankruptcy court, in San Antonio, Texas, was demanding stringent terms, though, so we halted negotiations.

But Office Depot, our biggest competitor, wanted the same stores. Just before the court was due to award the property in a sealed-bid auction, Vassalluzzo learned that Office Depot had negotiated a deal with Office Stop, subject to the court's approval. So he decided to make a dramatic, last-minute bid for the stores. He flew all night and, over Office Depot's loud objections, presented himself to the judge the next morning with a suitcase full of cash. "The judge was a riverboat gambler," says Vassalluzzo. "He said, 'They're here, they're real, and they have a bag full of money. They can participate in the auction.'" Within hours, we were declared the winner. It was an excellent offensive play. It prevented Office Depot from blocking us and at the same time enabled Staples to enter the Baltimore market with several stores at once.

The keep-away game gets tough when we sense intruders in markets where we have a major presence. In 1992, we got wind that OfficeMax hoped to enter the Boston metropolitan market by buying six stores from Highland Superstores, a failed electronics and appliance chain. Vassalluzzo and I were determined not to let it happen. We flew through a snowstorm to Detroit, where the chain was based, and met with Highland's chairman and head of real estate operations at 10:00 P.M. The past few days at Highland's offices had been quite heady as one CEO after another had visited in an effort to snag the stores. "Every day there's someone else," said the real estate executive. "What we have here is a very hot property."

As the meeting progressed, though, we learned that Highland's properties weren't what they originally thought. First, Highland insisted on selling the stores in a package. We did not want all of them. Second, and more important, the chain needed landlord consent to transfer the properties. They could not sublet the stores unless the landlord approved the new tenant. Vassalluzzo and I walked out of that meeting happy as clams. Rather than trying to negotiate with these guys, we decided we would just go after the stores we wanted—through the landlords, not through Highland. We visited the owners of Highland's Brighton, Weymouth, and Danvers stores and cut deals with them. If and when the owners got the sites back, we had them.

In the meantime, OfficeMax prematurely announced its pending triumph: It was coming to Boston with a six-store package purchased from Highland. A flurry of fearful analyst reports flew out of Wall Street. They said this would have a devastating impact on us— that we couldn't survive the first real competition we'd ever had in our home territory. OfficeMax didn't have long to gloat. When it tried to actually execute new leases on the three stores that we wanted, it confronted landlords who simply said, "Sorry. We want the store back."

That kind of trench warfare was instrumental. Office-Max ended up with a really lousy package of stores—one of which they've already closed—and paid big money for it, too. And we extracted the crown jewels from the package. Once again, the strategy paid double dividends. It expanded our territory while preventing a competitor from getting good locations. But it required some fancy footwork. We were able to simply convert one of the Highland stores. But the Weymouth, Massachusetts, space was adjacent to a shopping center in which we already had a store. So we moved into the Highland space and sublet the old space to a store that sold auto parts. We later decided we did not want the third location, so that was sublet to a computer superstore.

---

**HENRY FLIECK**
*Vice President of Real Estate*

When I joined Staples in 1990, everything was relatively manual in terms of site investigation. We used to literally take population counts by zip code. We worked out a somewhat analytical and somewhat seat-of-the-pants estimate of a prospective store's sales volume. We worked a lot of weekends and nights to get the math figured. Today if you draw a twelve-mile ring around a prospective store site, our computer will automatically diminish the volumes and population figures as you get further away from the store. We used to do that manually.

### REAL-LIFE LESSON

*The best defense is a good offense.*

Identify the central scarce resource in your business and scrap for it. At Staples, good real estate drives sales growth, protects us from competitors, and, sometimes, acts as a weapon against enemies. In your business, the resource might be information or craftsmanship. Find it, fight for it, and don't let your competitors get their hands on it.

# CHAPTER 5

# COMPETITION: FRIEND AND FOE

Within weeks after we opened our first store in 1986, Staples was making waves. Joe Antonini, chairman of Kmart, walked through the doors. And the word was that Wal-Mart executives had visited too. Charles Lazarus, the chairman of Toys "R" Us, who was also on Wal-Mart's board, attended a Wal-Mart board meeting at which Staples was described as the best new retail concept of the year. He passed the compliment on to Bob Nakasone, one of his managers and a Staples director. In the hypercompetitive field of retailing, any new experiment is worth checking out. It wasn't surprising that the retailing giants had come to inspect the store—the shock was that they had shown up so quickly!

The speed at which news of Staples had burst upon the retailing world would be a decisive factor in our success. If my superstore idea worked, we could expect other entrepreneurs and retailers to clone our store—but not for a year or so. Serious competition might not spring up until Staples went public, when its financials would be available for public consumption. That delay would grant us a giant head start, time in which to blanket key regions of the country with Staples stores. Being first might give us a chance to dominate the industry for decades.

> ## IN MY OWN WORDS
>
> Probably the one thing we did wrong we did by accident because we lived here. It's much tougher to do business in the Northeast than in the Sun Belt. It was a huge advantage for Office Depot that they started out without the obstacles of dealing with New York authorities and expensive media. Everything was cheaper down in Florida.

But this time it didn't work that way. The first imitator began ringing up sales five months after shopping carts had begun rolling through our Brighton store. Within two short years we, amazingly, had twenty competitors. But the proliferation did not occur because giants such as Home Depot and Wal-Mart charged after us. The force fueling the explosion of copycats was actually the venture capital community. Flush with cash from previous deals that had successfully gone public, venture capitalists were especially receptive to new retailing concepts. And to add fuel to the fire, two of my closest advisors helped put our most powerful competitor—Office Depot—on the map.

I asked Mike Grossman, founder of Grossman's Lumber, based in Braintree, Massachusetts, to serve on the Staples board because his experience operating a chain of home improvement stores would lend expertise and credibility with the venture capitalists. Not long after Grossman agreed, Pat Sher, an acquaintance, asked if he would act as a character reference. An entrepreneur who had cofounded Mr. How, a failed Home Depot clone, Sher was casting about for a new venture. Grossman agreed to be a reference. His support made Sher's enterprise—which turned out to be Office Depot—financeable.

Another Staples backer, Fred Adler, actually helped fill Office Depot's coffers. Just about the time our first store opened, Sher asked Adler to invest in Office Depot. Adler demurred, saying that he had a conflict of interest because he was a Staples investor. But he offered to refer the opportunity to another venture capitalist. Instead of calling an independent firm, the usual practice, he passed the deal to Joe Pagano,

## NO MEATCUTTERS AT STAPLES

I sat down with Bob (Nakasone) and ran through some of my logic on the numbers for the business: Here's what the Wholesale Club sells Post-it Notes for. This is what I would sell them for. Here's the volume Wholesale does in such and such a category, and here is the volume I think I can do in it. At the time the Wholesale Club was doing about $6 million a store.

In upstate New York, there was an outfit called Papercutter that was one-third office supply, one-third party supply, and one-third discount greeting cards. It was a hodgepodge. I told Bob what I thought I could do, what model Staples would follow, even what its payroll might look like. Both of us agreed that Staples' payroll would be lower than the typical grocer's because we wouldn't have to pay meatcutters. Bob and I worked through the model for the store. He gave me a lot of confidence because the more I listened to him, the more convinced I became that there was a business there.

an investment advisor from Aspen, Colorado. Pagano, however, was not a wholly independent third party. He managed the trusts of Adler's children.

Once they got wind of Adler's move, our other backers were angry. Bain's Romney and Bessemer's Hardymon flew to New York to confront Adler in his Park Avenue law offices. Adler, an aggressive corporate attorney legendary for his temper, was insulted and indignant. "Look," Adler protested, "there is no conflict of interest. It's only my children who are doing the investing in Office Depot." When Romney and Hardymon chided Adler over this excuse, he retorted, "It's none of your business. If you have a problem with it, talk to Tom."

As I prepared to meet with Adler, I got a cautionary call from one of his partners. He said, "Fred's about to explode over this. The secretaries are diving for cover." Sure enough, when I walked into Adler's office, I found a volcano primed to erupt. Adler was sitting in his customary spot, a leather desk chair that elevated him several inches higher than anyone else seated in his office. As I sat gazing up at him, Adler let it loose. There was no conflict of inter-

---

**BO CHEADLE**
*Securities Analyst at*
*Montgomery Securities*

Staples pursued a fortress strategy. It determined that if it were successful, it would attract a lot of competitors. So it entered into high-cost markets and built relatively small stores—to lessen the need for capital and lower operating costs. However, what Staples didn't factor in was that the money would flow into the business so rapidly that the cycle would be compressed. A cycle that would normally have taken ten years was squeezed into two or three years. What caused that change was technology and the venture capitalists' huge appetite for new retail concepts. So everybody got into the business. Then it obviously became much more difficult.

est, he insisted. *He* wasn't investing in Office Depot. Besides, he didn't like taking orders. Bain was an unseasoned venture cap-ital firm. "What the hell is a snotpicker like Romney telling me what to do?" he screamed. As for Hardymon, continued the lawyer, he'd been hanging around with uptight Yankees too long. He just would not be treated this way. "You mess with me and you know what? I'm going to crush you!" he angrily concluded, pulling a legal pad off of his desk and crushing it between his hands.

Having a well-financed competitor was worrisome, but what was especially dis-

> ### TODD KRASNOW
>
> By building these networks [of stores] in these big markets like New York and Boston we have been able to make it difficult for the competition to thrive. Office Depot came to metro New York only in late 1995. They're not in New York with any meaningful pres-ence, they're not in Boston, and they're not in Philadelphia or any-where in between. One of the reasons is we have a very, very good network, and it's really tough to steal customers from a direct competitor when you don't have the economies of adver-tising leverage.

heartening was that Office Depot had it so easy. Where we were forced to laboriously invent Staples from scratch, Office Depot breezed into the business by copying every-thing we did. Krasnow explains, "They didn't have to do any research. Their early positioning was simply to go to ven-dors and say, 'Whatever you're selling to Staples, sell to us.' So they got started in half the time that it took us."

The Florida start-up was such an unabashed imitator that it even copied our mistakes. One of our first market-ing brochures, for example, contained a typo. Shopping at Staples, it declared, was "hassel-free." When Office Depot had its own marketing literature printed up, its managers didn't even bother to correct the spelling. Shopping at Office Depot, its hot-off-the-presses brochure boasted, was "hassel-free" too.

As Staples and Office Depot began to demonstrate that selling office supplies in a superstore was tremendously profitable, venture capitalists began to scramble over each other to get a piece of the future fortune. "You could see that Staples was clearly going to be a success and there was an enormous market out there. Those venture capitalists who didn't participate in Staples or Office Depot started throwing money at other clones," says Bo Cheadle, a securities analyst at Montgomery Securities. By the end of 1988, Office Depot had 26 stores to Staples' 22, Office Club had opened 15, BizMart had established 10, and OfficeMax had launched fewer than a dozen. More than a dozen other clones, including WORKplace, HQ Office Supplies Warehouse, HQ International, Office World, and Office Place, each had two to seven stores in place. Small surprise, then, that when I was asked in 1989 how it felt to be the father of the office-supplies superstore industry, I replied, "I wish I had worn a condom."

---

### ON IMITATORS AND COMPETITORS

Our competitors quickly mimicked well-known discount retailers and stole some of their luster. Office Depot's name was a direct copy of Home Depot.

Every time Office Depot went to a market where Home Depot was well known, people immediately thought it was a Home Depot for the office. Office Club opened in California where everybody goes to the Price Club. But what was Staples? It was a real negative at first. As time has passed, people have gotten to know us, and now most of them think that we have a nifty name. It is distinctive because everybody else is Office *Something*. But we are Staples.

---

### REAL-LIFE LESSON

*You can't keep competitors away from a good idea.*

Few businesses make copycatting as easy as retailing. But any superior business concept—or improvement on a concept—will draw better-financed, more powerful competitors. Confidentiality agreements mean nothing. If you're successful, you can't prevent others from trying to enter your domain. But you can focus your energies on executing your idea better than could anyone else.

---

## The Upside: Cherry-Picking Competitors' Best Ideas

Though they were imitating my basic idea, the Staples clones were not identical. We were trying to build a critical mass of stores in the Northeast to shut out competitors and make it cost-effective to advertise in the region's high-cost media. Office Depot, in Florida, had larger stores than we did and plenty of money to advertise heavily and expand quickly. Office Club, which was run by Mark Begelman, a former furniture retailing executive, was modeled after Price Club, the grocery wholesale chain. Launched in California, its stores charged customers to become members and carried fewer items but offered prices even lower than ours.

While the differences were troubling—because they forced us to reexamine our strategy—they were also exciting.

For the first time, we could scrutinize other retailers' ideas—and filch the best ones. "Some of the chains were ahead of their time in being very consumer-friendly. In 1988, the home market wasn't what it is today. These chains didn't have the bread-and-butter business customer, but they came up with interesting ways to display product and design their stores," says Krasnow.

As we knew, gathering intelligence on the competition could be as simple as visiting a store. But at first, our own view of the world prevented us from appreciating alternative approaches. In 1987, I sent two managers to Florida to study Office Depot's first four stores. Posing as customers, they walked through every aisle, studying Office Depot employees, estimating the number of items being sold, and comparing prices. Their first overwhelming impression: The stores were a mess. Packaging littered the floor, boxes of goods had been ripped open, merchandise tickets were missing, and store shelves had big empty spaces where items had been sold out. The duo did not find it hard to reach a conclusion. "They said Office Depot was never going to make it," remembers Krasnow.

---

### EXCERPT FROM A MEMO ASSESSING OFFICE DEPOT'S STORES

"They make very little effort in the areas of customer service. We asked a number of questions of various employees at [sic] which we received fair to poor responses. They appeared indifferent and basically uninformed. In the area of service to the consumer, it simply came down to our having consultants, management, and employees in general trained and available to assist the customer where Office Depot had a work force designed to strictly [sic] deal with product packout and display.... [Stock] maintenance was quite poor in all locations. Many items out of stock, shelves not straightened, *(continued)*

In fact, Office Depot not only "made it," the Florida clone outstripped Staples, becoming the largest office-supplies retailer in the country, with an estimated $5.5 billion in 1995 sales. So what happened? "In hindsight, what the ripped boxes and messy stores reflected was that their prices were really, really good," explains Krasnow. "Customers were snapping up merchandise. Office Depot had challenges that needed to be overcome, but the basic demand was there. And it obviously became very, very successful."

Not long afterward, we got a lesson in how willing competitors were to take espionage activities to the extreme. In 1988, we were preparing to open our Springfield, Virginia, store. It was located in a mall in which Montgomery Ward was an anchor. The mall was open, but our store was still under construction. A wall divided Staples from Montgomery Ward, which happened to own a stake in Office World, one of our competitors. We had no reason to give Montgomery Ward's relationship to Office World a second thought until several days before the Springfield grand opening. As managers and associates were busily setting up merchandise in the new space, they were startled to see a stranger filming the store with a video camera. Obviously the man had climbed the dividing wall to gain entry. Several Staples associates quickly

and shelf tags that were missing, outdated, and in wrong locations. . . .We personally felt much better about our operation and were not impressed by their lack of standards and personnel. If we were to put a store up against them there's no doubt we would be much superior."

This memo is a perfect example of how easily you can be blinded by your own self-confidence. When you go to somebody else's store, the last thing you want to discuss is how the competitor is screwing up. You want to find out what those guys do better than you.

extracted the tape from the camera and escorted the man out of the mall.

The message was clear: Spy or be spied upon. Staples executives lost no time in poring over other chains' techniques and innovations. I used to shop with my mother-in-law. She had an apartment in Fort Lauderdale, and together we put the nearest Office Depot store through its paces. She'd order paper clips, pens, and paper to be delivered to her apartment, and then call to complain and ask that the stuff be picked up and returned to the store. I really wanted to learn how they did everything: what their systems were like, what they had in stock, and what they couldn't do. I visited stores constantly.

On another occasion, I had my wife, Dola, apply for a job at Office Depot's Atlanta delivery-order center. She said she had experience in telemarketing and, in a soft, Southern accent, explained that she was anxious to move back "home." Staples did not offer delivery service at the time, so I wanted to investigate how Office Depot's delivery system worked, how many people were in the operation, and how it trained employees. Dola stopped the application process before the company even offered her a job interview, but we still got the information.

## BIG COMPETITORS IN A (RELATIVELY) SMALL MARKET

I was worried about Sears, Kmart, and other big companies coming after us. In fact some of them did, but none of them turned out to be a viable threat. Office Max wasn't a Kmart start-up, although Kmart financed it. They never actually ran it, however. Other big names looked our way: International Paper, Ben Franklin Stores, Ames, and Montgomery Ward, but none of those guys made it in our business. And that's quite a list!

Some of our sleuthing seemed more like a scene from Laurel and Hardy than James Bond. During a visit to Florida, five executives, including Krasnow, visited Office Depot's North Miami Beach store. While scouring the facility for information, Krasnow noticed the employee schedule posted on a bulletin board and quickly made a mental note of all the pertinent numbers. Fifteen minutes later, the Staples executives were preparing to leave when they heard a commotion. One of the Staples executives was racing down an aisle, waving a piece of paper in his hand and crying, "I got the schedule! I got the schedule!" Behind him, a half-dozen Office Depot associates were in hot pursuit. "It was the same report that I saw," says Krasnow. "We all bolted out of the store and ran to the parking lot."

### REAL-LIFE LESSON

*Never underestimate your competitors.*

It's all too easy to believe that your strategy is superior to a competitor's. You've chosen it because you believe in it. But underestimating your competitors can only hurt you. Even the worst of them probably has one or two ideas from which you could benefit. And you can be sure they're poring over your approach, too. Scrapping for competitive information is vital when you're small.

# Changing Alliances: Redrawing the Battlefield

"Retail is detail" is one of my guiding mottos. But as the superstore chains began to grow, our need for market intelligence shifted. Now we needed to learn about competitors' plans as well as store operations. In 1989, we heard that Office Warehouse would be entering the Philadelphia market. Vassalluzzo and I were traveling around the region with a broker, wondering where its sites were—and if they were any good. The next day the broker obligingly reported where Office Warehouse planned to locate its stores. "How do you know?" demanded Vassalluzzo.

"Easy," said the broker. "I just called Larry Pacey." Pacey was a marketing executive who had left Office Depot to work at Office Warehouse. "I posed as a reporter from the *Philadelphia Business Journal* and said we wanted to do a story on his opening in Philadelphia and, particularly, on his new sites," continued the broker. Pacey told the broker that the information was sensitive, but that he would check to see if he could release the information because the company might want the publicity. Permission granted. We now knew where all sites were, so we checked them out. It turned out the locations were just awful.

Hot competition transformed some friendships into enmity. I had formed a close relationship with Mark Begelman, CEO of Office Club in California, almost from that company's inception in 1987. Begelman hadn't conceived the idea for Office Club—he had been recruited from the furniture store industry to office-supplies retailing by venture capitalists eager to get a piece of the hot new concept. But he adapted beautifully. "He really understands the nuts and bolts of retailing, store presentation, visual merchandising, and advertising," says Steve Westerfield, who was running WORKplace at the time.

With Staples on the East Coast and Office Club on the West Coast, normal competitive instincts were muffled. Begelman and I attended each other's store openings, got to know each other's wives, and traded ideas. We were somewhat cautious. We didn't open the kimonos all the way, but we would compare notes on how to compete with Office Depot—who was our common enemy.

Then Staples received a flood of capital when we went public. After watching Office Depot operate so effortlessly in its low-cost markets, we made a momentous decision: We would enter the Los Angeles market. Office Depot was doing so well because they could afford to advertise heavily. They were in cheap markets. I couldn't buy the *New York Times* or New York *Newsday*. Those guys could go to Orlando and buy newspaper

**TODD KRASNOW**

Looking back, the market was so much bigger than anybody thought it was going to be that we probably invested way more energy than we should have in worrying about competitors. The industry has proven to be one of the best segments of retailing that there is, with loads of opportunity for everyone. That we were worrying about each other when we had three Staples stores and they had two Office Depot stores, with hindsight, was the wrong thing to pay attention to.

advertisements dirt cheap, and bang—open three stores. But costs on the West Coast were as high as they were on the East Coast. We hoped to create another "fortress" there. We entered L.A., and that was the end of my friendship with Begelman. He hated me for it.

REAL-LIFE LESSON

*The lines of battle change constantly.*

Territory is everything in our business. Even if the borders in your business aren't the kind that can be drawn on a map, they exist. Do not assume they won't be infringed upon by competitors—or that you can't cross them yourself. And don't assume your relationships will stay the same if the boundaries change.

# CHAPTER 6

# NEW YORK AND OTHER FOREIGN CITIES

Strictly speaking, Staples didn't become an international company until 1993. But we learned how to enter strange lands with foreign customs by opening stores in the daunting city of New York. "The retail real estate market in North America is in many ways a jungle—and in New York it's a heightened jungle," says Joe Vassalluzzo. All the rules that applied to real estate transactions in New England were suspended in the Big Apple.

Landlords in New York run the gamut in race, religion, and disposition. Myra Hart, Staples' first head of real estate operations, remembers trying to negotiate for a derelict property owned by Iranians. Though they were all sitting at the same table, she could not get the Iranians to speak to her during the negotiations. "They would address everything to the men," she recalls. To reach an agreement, she had to periodically ask the landlords to leave the room, so that she could direct her male colleagues about handling the discussions.

Our Manhattan leases taught us the first dictum of going global: When in alien territory, adapt to local customs. Hart, Leo Kahn, and I were reviewing the terms of one of the Manhattan deals in the Sixth Avenue office of Al Goldberg, our prospective landlord. Goldberg's assistant was Ralph Marx, a gruff, cigar-chomping man who did not speak without Goldberg's permission. Hart asked how long it would take to get a permit.

Marx looked at Goldberg. Goldberg nodded. Marx turned to face us. "Rocko and Joe can get it for us in two to three weeks," he said in a heavy New York accent.

Hart was puzzled. "Excuse me, who's Rocko and who's Joe?" she asked.

Marx looked at Goldberg. Goldberg nodded. Rolling a cigar from side to side in his mouth, Marx answered, "They're architectural expediters."

Hart didn't like the sound of that. "No, you don't understand," she protested. "We're going to be a public company. We can't do anything close to breaking the law."

After a few minutes of listening to her objections, Goldberg leaned over and said in a condescending tone, "Toots, you don't understand how things get done in New York."

Affronted, Hart was about to jump to her feet when Kahn and I grabbed her arms to restrain her. Kahn leaned over and asked, "Tell me this now. How long would it take us—or would we even get a permit—if we didn't use an 'architectural expediter'?"

Marx looked expectantly at Goldberg. Goldberg nodded. "Oh, about three years," said Marx.

At that point Kahn decided to strike a compromise. "Hey listen, Ralph . . . Al . . . what say you hire Rocko, you pay Rocko, and we pay you?" he suggested.

Adjusting to foreign customs does not mean caving on key negotiating points, however. I remember flying to New York to meet with another potential landlord. As he and his real estate broker walked into the office building, the broker turned and said, "You know, I think the Mob may be the landlord here." After we concluded the meeting, Jack, the landlord, handed me a business card with an unfamiliar company name on it.

"What's this?" I asked.

"The family," intoned Jack.

"Which family?" I wondered

"No, you idiot," roared Jack. "The family!"

Negotiations for the space later bogged down over the actual square footage involved. Because I knew the store from its earlier incarnation as a Finast supermarket, I knew the space measured 14,300 square feet—but Jack's documents described it as 15,000 square feet. Finally, I called Jack to say that we would pay rent only on the actual space.

"Look, the family thinks it's 15,000 square feet. You know?" Jack answered. "I'll make it 15,000 square feet for the rent we agreed on, or we can raise the rent on a lower square footage. Take your pick."

"Jack, you know we just can't do that. We've got banks involved in this. It's a fair rent for your building," I said.

"Okay. Can we split the difference and call it fourteen-six?" Jack asked.

I stuck to my guns and at the end of the day got the store for the agreed-upon rent—on 14,300 square feet.

New Yorkers' priorities were often wonderfully bizarre. In 1992, two supermarket entrepreneurs joined forces to buy a property in the Bay Ridge area of Brooklyn that had previously housed a supermarket. Though they were fierce competitors, the two characters wanted to ensure that this property would never, ever again become a supermarket. So they began negotiating to lease it to Staples. Early one morning, Joe Vassalluzzo showed up at a spartan, musty Manhattan office to meet with them. It was early, so he asked for some coffee. That triggered a major argument. The coffee pot was broken and if the sole receptionist/secretary left the office to buy coffee, there would be no one to answer the phone. To Vassalluzzo's amazement, the two self-made entrepreneurs began to argue vehemently about who would go and who would pay. "We had a 30-minute debate about coffee," remembers Vassalluzzo.

At that meeting the supermarket entrepreneurs insisted that their attorney be the scrivener. Vassalluzzo agreed. But within a few weeks of his return to Framingham, negotiations began to bog down. Why? The attorney was sick. Vassalluzzo was skeptical. "A lot of times during negotiations there are hidden agendas," he explains. "So whenever something doesn't make sense, you have to question it." As the months wore on, and the attorney's illness continued to be the ostensible reason for the delay, Vassalluzzo and his team questioned the explanation so often that even the supermarket owners began to doubt whether their attorney was sick.

Finally, nine months after negotiations had started, the transaction was consummated. Normally, you do not hear from a landlord after the lease is signed. But one day Vassalluzzo received a call from one of the owners. "Remember all the months that the attorney was sick?" he asked Vassalluzzo. Well, the attorney had died. The New Yorker paused. Then he reflected soberly about how important it was for everyone to remember to stop and smell the roses in life. Joe had no sooner murmured his agreement than the landlord, without missing a beat, began to rake Vassalluzzo over the coals regarding a tax bill. "I said, 'Wait a minute. What about smelling the roses?'" says Vassalluzzo with a laugh.

The other owner was equally proficient at ingratiating himself to us while serving his own interests. He called Vassalluzzo one day and asked if we had noticed any missing trolleys. After finally realizing that the supermarket owner was

### WAY DOWN SOUTH IN DIXIE

I often wonder whether we should not have moved into the Sunbelt sooner than we did. Many of our competitors had chosen to go that route, but for a while we had staked out the Northeast. The South was one of the last regions we entered, despite its advantages. Especially when you have low taxes and low rents, suddenly your cash flow problems don't look so huge. In many sunbelt towns—Greenville, South Carolina, and Greensboro, North Carolina—your costs for rent and taxes are so low that the retail business really has a chance to thrive. It's a great region.

talking about shopping carts, Vassalluzzo demurred, saying that he wasn't in a position to know. "Well," the supermarket owner informed him as though he were doing Vassalluzzo a huge favor, "one of our employees has been stealing trolleys from Staples. We are going to terminate the employee and return the trolleys to you," the supermarket owner continued.

"Gee," said Vassalluzzo. "That's very nice of you."

"I just want you to know I'm doing you a service," the entrepreneur replied. Then he added, almost as an afterthought, "Yeah, our meat manager was stealing meat from the supermarket and using your carts to carry it away." That, Vassalluzzo came to believe, was how New Yorkers defined selflessness.

On another occasion, Staples was pursuing a former disco on Queens Boulevard. Joe, the owner, was having difficulty relating to Katherine McGlade, one of our real estate directors. He wanted to make a special demand, man to man, so he invited Henry Flieck, head of real estate, to an evening of women's mud wrestling. Flieck declined, so Joe, a balding, well-dressed man in his forties, made his pitch to Flieck after dinner in a dark Queens restaurant instead. What he needed was money—$500,000. Normally, a tenant is not required to make a down payment on a lease. But Joe was tormented for reasons he did not explain and wanted cash from us.

"Look, we've got to sign today," Joe wheedled, leaning over the table. "I don't care if we sign—just give me even $100,000 today. Henry, we're friends. We ate together. We drank together. We have a relationship. I need the money today."

"It was like a scene out of a Scorsese movie. He literally wanted a huge cash payment with no security," recalls Vassalluzzo. We did not give him the money, and the former disco became a Korean food market.

Some of Staples' most memorable New York moments came out of a relationship with one of the country's largest and most successful real estate entrepreneurs. Vassalluzzo first met this powerful landlord regarding a lease we had purchased in northern New Jersey back when Staples was still a smallish company. The ostensible reason for the meeting was to discuss the possibility of selling the lease back to the landlord, an arrangement the landlord favored because it would give him more control.

The real reason was that Vassalluzzo, who had recently joined Staples, would try to get a major concession from the landlord: renewal options. Thus far the landlord's company had not granted us the standard option to renew the lease after ten years at our own discretion. "I was there to demonstrate that Staples had made a tremendous commitment to its growth program by recruiting high-level professionals and that Staples was a serious player," says Vassalluzzo. "All of which meant nothing to this guy."

The landlord did not listen to anything Vassalluzzo had to say. Instead he began to talk about the nice relationship building between Staples and his own organization. He mentioned the number of deals they had made together. Then, seemingly talking to his chief operating officer, who was also in the room, the landlord mentioned a property in another spot in New Jersey. "Oh, West Paterson," he exclaimed to his associate while keeping his eyes locked on Vassalluzzo. "That's the lease where we can throw them out any time we want!"

Being terminated at the landlord's will is the last thing any tenant wants—and it would be humiliating for us to have to accept such a condition. The landlord knew Vassalluzzo was new. "He wanted to see what kind of a reaction I would have. I was floored, but I said, 'I can't believe you have a right to do that. I haven't read the lease, but it would be startling to me if that were true,'" recalls Vassalluzzo. After holding his ground in the meeting, Vassalluzzo was surprised on his return to Framingham to find that if he terminated all the tenants in the mall, the landlord did indeed have the right to terminate the Staples lease, too.

## REAL-LIFE LESSON

### Doing business in foreign cities is foreign.

It's obvious, but no one is really prepared when it happens to them. To accomplish anything in an alien culture, you'll have to bend at least a few rules. The trick is to know which principles you are willing to amend and which you aren't—and why.

# Going International: An Unnecessary Diversion?

While we coped with the mad rush of clones in the U.S., a Canadian businessman was beginning to picture a chain of office-supplies superstores in his country. As president of Beaver Lumber, which was owned by the Molson brewing company, Jack Bingleman had in 1989 initiated a large research project that evaluated the prospects of starting a Home Depot–like chain in Canada. Molson ultimately launched a home-center chain, which was later sold to Home Depot. But from the beginning, Bingleman was more strongly attracted to the idea of super-large discount stores than to the home-center business. "In the process of doing the research, I became extremely convinced that big-box category killers were going to play a big role in the future, and I became interested in the idea as both a retailer and an investor," recalls Bingleman. He did not have to look far to see what kind of product might work in the superstore setting. Molson also owned one of Canada's two largest office-supplies chains. That business was a creature of the past, as Bingleman saw it: inefficient, with high-priced merchandise.

Bingleman was so excited about the opportunity that in 1990 he quit Beaver to research the new business. He also contacted Staples, Office Club, and Office Depot, hoping to plug into a proven formula that was up and running. After Mike Grossman, one of Staples' first directors, introduced him to me, Bingleman felt he'd found his corporate sponsor. "I liked Staples, and in particular I liked it because they did business adjacent to Canada and had distribution facilities that were somewhat close to the Canadian border."

But did we like Bingleman and his idea? You bet. I had no ambivalence about the opportunity that he was presenting. Here was Bingleman, an experienced, successful retailer, who wanted to be the first office-supplies superstore chain in Canada, just as Staples had been in the U.S. Bingleman wanted us to share our expertise, but he was willing to finance his start-up without us. What did we have to lose by supporting him?

The board, however, felt quite differently. Staples had only about 35 stores, and the competition from clones was fierce. We had opportunities aplenty in our own country— the total market was beginning to look as if it could hit $100 billion. Canada's market was only about $10 billion. The last thing we needed was to divert capital and energy to a start-up in another country, argued Dave Lubrano and other board members. I refused to give up, and finally, in late 1990, the board agreed to a tentative first step: We would split the research costs with Bingleman while he developed a business plan that could be used to raise capital and recruit talent. After the business plan was written, we would decide whether to invest.

By the time Bingleman was finished with his plan, the board agreed to invest $2 million for 16-percent ownership of the Canadian's business. During the first half of 1991, Goldman Sachs lined up 25 individual and institutional investors willing to put up $10 million. By fall, the company, named Business Depot, was ready to open its first store.

Our first baby step into globalization was tremendously useful in laying the groundwork for future cross-border expansion. Though the Canadian market was very similar to its U.S. counterpart, it was different enough that we had to learn how to amend our U.S. blueprint for success. "Ninety-five percent of what you do and the way customers respond in Canada is the same as the U.S.," says Bingleman. "But you can get into a lot of trouble with the other 5 percent."

Take the simple logistics of getting the product into the stores. Canada is a country in which everyone lives one hundred miles from the U.S. border that stretches 3,500 miles from coast to coast. Everything moves east and west. In the U.S., by contrast, things move north, south, east, west, and in circles. That single difference dictated an array of differences in how Business Depot would operate. It meant Bingleman's operation required a completely different distribution system than Staples'. It was also a key factor in electing whether to use local, regional, or national advertising.

There were myriad other differences, too. Two languages are spoken in Canada. What's more, electrical equipment requires a different approval process. According to Bingleman,

"Canadian managers are more intuitive than Americans. Americans are far more analytical. The reason for that is that if you want to be a national chain in Canada, you have to operate in a market like Toronto, where there are four million people, and you have to operate in little communities in Saskatchewan, where there are two thousand people. You can't put the Coke machine in the same place in every store, because they're so different."

But perhaps the most important element of our Canadian experiment is that we learned how crucial a strong relationship is to international operations. Staples' success in the U.S., and the proliferation of competitors, had fostered a cookie-cutter approach to fast growth. For the first time, we had to live with a partner, Bingleman, who had a strong point of view, too. Although we were very much in the driver's seat because we had the expertise and clout in banking, leasing, and legal matters, we were forced to develop methods to share—and receive—information. "You learn how to manage these relationships because you probably need the relationship to understand what the country is all about, what the culture is all about, and how to do business," explains Bingleman.

My decision to sponsor Business Depot was richly rewarded. Business Depot stores usually began turning a profit within ten months of opening. Within two and a half years, the company had nearly thirty stores and began to produce earnings. By 1994, its share of the Canadian office-supplies market surpassed that of Grand and Toy, the previous industry leader. We had been boosting our share of ownership in the intervening years, and we decided to buy the rest of Business Depot. "The Canadian operation was more successful than Office

Depot or OfficeMax in its formative years because of the advice Staples gave it," says Westerfield. "Jack worked unrelentingly and the company has gained such strong control of the Canadian market that if anybody wants to be a meaningful competitor up there, it will be costly for them."

## REAL-LIFE LESSON

### *Think three steps ahead.*

With perspective, particularly 20/20 hindsight, everything seems clear. But sometimes being swamped by the particulars of a current business can give you extraordinary foresight. Being in the midst of a battle for dominance of the U.S. market allowed me to see how to wage that war even more successfully in another country. There I could execute the concept even better—raising more money sooner, blanketing the country faster, and forestalling competitors more effectively. In pondering the shape of the battle outside the U.S., somewhere in the distant future, I found myself thinking three steps ahead. If I had limited my thinking to the all-consuming present, Staples would have never become Canada's industry leader.

# Speed Bumps on the Transatlantic Highway

Our forays into Canada brought a dazzlingly seductive issue before the board: foreign expansion. None of our rivals had stepped foot in other countries yet. If we charged ahead, Staples could dominate the industry in other countries. The board was also concerned about sales growth. After presenting shareholders with 50 percent annual sales growth, what would we do for an encore once the U.S. market was saturated with office-supplies superstores?

The answer seemed to point to Europe. The U.K., for example, seemed ripe for the Staples concept. Individual and business customers were being served by small, high-priced mom-and-pop shops offering little service. But there was no Jack Bingleman setting up a chain in Britain. What we needed was a corporate partner in the U.K. According to Joe Vassalluzzo, "You absolutely cannot do it yourself. There are too many cultural impediments for you to know where the booby traps lie. In a retail start-up, the most important task is to generate locations. There's no way a U.S. national can go into any country and generate the real estate it needs. That person will be chasing his tail for a long time." In 1992, after

## TODD KRASNOW

I went to a closing in Germany that shows you how big the cultural differences are. I took the red-eye, flew all night, didn't sleep particularly much, and then went to their offices. For some reason the office buildings in Hamburg don't have particularly good ventilation, and it seems like everybody smokes in Germany. We went into this room. Under German law the documents have to be read out loud before you can sign them. So, we had to stay for six hours in a smoke-filled room, with only little biscuits to eat and wine to drink. I'm twenty-eighth hour of being awake. *(continued)* months of research and networking, we joined forces with Kingfisher, PLC, a large U.K. retailer that operates home improvement, consumer electronics, and Woolworth chains.

Because both countries are English-speaking, the temptation is to believe that there will be few impediments to transferring a U.S. business to the U.K. But, in Vassalluzzo's estimation, George Bernard Shaw was right: "The U.S. and Britain are two great countries separated by a common language." Vassalluzzo remembers the day that he overheard a U.K. associate talking to a Staples associate about turnover. The Staples associate grew more and more perplexed until Vassalluzzo interrupted to clarify matters. In the U.S. "turnover" refers to "employee churn." In Britain, it means "sales." Says Vassalluzzo, "Multiply that misunderstanding a hundred times and you have some idea of what it's like—and that's in a country with the same language."

Then came the closing dinner. Wolfgang Friederichsen, our gregarious host and new partner, brought us to a restaurant in a nice section of Hamburg, and the first course that came around was a soup. It was just a broth, and the first thing the waiter did was crack an egg into each one. The soup was not warm enough for the egg to cook—it was just sitting there. Then they came around and scraped these little red things into the soup. It was bone marrow. This is like 9:00 at night, so I'm famished. Then the main course came, which had been ordered for us. It was a house specialty: pig knuckles. I am so tired because I have not had a chance to take out my contact lenses, and my eyes feel like they're going to fall out of my head. Our German partners are wonderful people and great friends of ours, but it is a wholly different culture, and you don't think of it as being that different. It just shows how jet lag and cultural differences can make more of an impact than you might imagine.

Nevertheless, results from Staples U.K.'s four pilot stores have justified the expansion. While they're still not profitable, revenues are stronger than expected. So in 1996 we will bring a total of 35 U.K. stores online, hoping to snare a significant portion of the country's $10 billion market before Globus, our only rival, expands its presence.

Our decision to enter Germany in 1992 was guided by what seemed like a custom-made opportunity: a chance to buy into MAXI-Papier, a clone company that was copying what we had done in the U.S. The German company's first store was doing well. We said, "Look, let's just buy into their business with the rights to step up our ownership over time."

No sooner were the papers signed than the problems began to mount. Subsequent stores were established in poor locations and did not perform as well. The stores themselves were, on average, 14,000 square feet and carried 4,000 items. The smaller size and limited selection robbed MAXI-Papier stores of some of the key features offered by their U.S. cousins. But even more important, business conditions in Germany are positively daunting for a retailer touting low prices and convenience. The country prohibits companies from offering a coupon worth more than about twenty-five cents. It is illegal to say that you have guaranteed low prices. Retailers are not allowed to be open after

> ### IN MY OWN WORDS
>
> When things don't work out, a leader should be willing to take the blame. Most people running companies could do it. It's a wonderful leadership technique. So many companies are absorbed with covering up their mistakes and rationalizing their bad decisions. It's just much better to say, "Hey we screwed that one up. Next." When Germany was going badly, I made a big point of making Germany my project. It would have been very easy to slough it off and blame everybody else. By saying, "Hey, we tried Germany. Right now it's not working. Let's own up to it. Let's deal with it," we made it pretty clear that it's not the end of the world to try something and have it fail.

6:00 P.M. except on Thursdays. "We can't do many of the things that have worked for us in the U.S. So how do you build your business?" asks Todd Krasnow.

Our natural response to MAXI-Papier's troubles was to try something gutsy, and if that didn't work, try something else. But here is where cultural differences began to seem like impenetrable walls. "From their perspective, Americans change their mind all the time about everything. They think we should just slow down and in five years we'll have a very nice business," explains Krasnow. Each partner also believes his own expertise should dictate the course of the business. They think we don't understand their market. We'd send guys over on joint venture teams to accomplish X, Y, and Z and the German guys would say, "Oh, yeah, we'll do that, sure." Then after the team went home they'd say, "Should we do it? Nah, . . . they won't be back for awhile."

The copy center debate was a key example. None of the stores that we inherited when we bought a 48-percent interest in MAXI-Papier had copy machines available to customers. They had always been a successful component of our U.S. stores, so we naturally suggested that copy centers be introduced in Germany. "The managing director said there is no way the German customer is interested in using copy centers," remembers Vassalluzzo. But after months and months of negotiations, we prevailed. MAXI-Papier would test a center. The result? It was an immediate success.

Such victories were too few, though. By mid-1994, the board was considering writing off its investment in MAXI-Papier. In the end, however, Vassalluzzo and I decided to extend the experiment with new management. We brought in

Peter von le Fort as managing director. He was one of the original investors in MAXI-Papier and former chief operating officer of Max Bahr, one of Germany's leading home improvement chains. We also promoted Michael Bauer, a German national trained by both IKEA and Staples in the U.S., to operations controller of the German operation. While the moves have improved our ability to implement new ideas, we do not expect our German stores to generate significant earnings until the end of the '90s.

## REAL-LIFE LESSON

*A solid working relationship is more important than any other factor to being successful in international markets.*

An overseas business must pass other criteria, of course. But an international venture won't fly just because, for example, the market for low-priced office supplies is big and untapped. You need a partner with whom you can truly work well. Sometimes the only way to be sure of that is to insist that one partner be in the driver's seat. "I don't know if a 50/50 joint venture is the way to go. There has to be one decisive party at the end of the day," says Joe Vassalluzzo.

# CHAPTER 7

# RACE OF THE RETAILERS

Though we had been invaded by an army of clones early in life, we did not feel the heat of competition until we broke into the Southern California market with four stores in 1990. With eight stores already established, Office Club, our leading competitor in the market, was hardly likely to ignore this incursion into its territory. Moreover, Mark Begelman, Office Club's CEO and onetime ally of mine, felt betrayed by our entry into his territory. A conflagration was inevitable.

But at first we ignored Office Club. Instead, we were scrutinizing Price Club. Though it was a warehouse store selling food and general merchandise, not a Staples-style store, Price Club had the largest share of the office-supplies market in California. So our marketing campaign focused tightly on the advantages of shopping at Staples over Price Club: We had the same low prices but more merchandise and no membership fee. "What we failed to realize was that Price Club was very worried about Office Club—and was pricing against Office Club," says Krasnow. "So when we went and matched Price Club, we were matching Office Club. And Office Club was saying, 'We're not going to let anybody have the same price as us.'"

The war began. Office Club lowered its prices, causing Price Club to drop its prices. We, in turn, followed Price Club down. Begelman could tolerate Price Club having the same prices as his company, but not Staples. So he knocked prices down again. And on and on it went. "It was one of those terrifying plunges, where prices just kept going down and down and down, and in reality, there was no particular reason for it," remembers Krasnow. The price war drove margins down by a steep 7 or 8 percent.

The grand irony: The pain was entirely self-inflicted by all three stores. Price Club had ten area locations, but only around 200 office-supply items. Between us, Staples and Office Club had just twelve stores in all of Southern California. We were so new to the market that there was plenty of business for everyone. We were just beginning to take market share away from stationery stores and dealers. Retail customers were just beginning to discover us. There was very little chance that customers would drive from one store to another because of a small price difference. No matter where we stood in relation to each other, all the prices looked good to customers, who had been paying 100 percent more!

After three or four months, we finally came to our senses. "We realized by engaging in this price war, we were focusing on our competitors, not our customers. Our customers weren't paying attention to this spat," says Krasnow. So with great trepidation, we raised our prices a little. "You feel like you're just doing the absolute wrong thing, because your whole position is: We have the lowest price," says Krasnow. But Office Club and Price Club followed, and the cycle reversed itself. Eventually the three companies carved out different price niches, each unwilling to be undercut on twenty or so top-selling items.

## TODD KRASNOW

The notion of fighting with each other over price is actually kind of ludicrous. But at the time you're intent on establishing yourself and not letting any competitor get any headway. There was no particular reason to lower prices from a competitive point of view, but it was a very difficult process to break. That price-cutting cycle repeated itself several times early on as competitors converged in different parts of the country. Every time it happened there would be this drop, drop, drop, drop, and then it would start to go back up, leveling out at prices slightly below where they started. We in the industry didn't get more rational until 1992. We finally realized that it's not in any company's self-interest to have a price war because you can get lots of market share without having a price war. And having a price war among low-priced competitors doesn't get you more market share. It didn't serve any purpose.

REAL-LIFE LESSON

*There can be more than one winner.*

The heat of competition can cause you to concentrate on your enemies instead of your customers. We were tearing the profits out of our businesses when we did not need to. Today there are 130 office-supplies superstores prospering in Southern California. Some belong to us, some to others. If the market is big enough, there is room for more than one winner.

## Guerrilla Warfare

Plentiful as business was for the newly hatched office-supplies chains, some fights with competitors had to be fought. In an incident well known in the industry, Steve Westerfield, the former CEO of WORKplace, who eventually sold his company to Staples, was forced into waging battle with Office Depot. WORKplace was a clone that had built up a strong presence in California and Florida not long after Staples began operating. But it was so undercapitalized that by 1989 it was forced into selling assets. "Already Staples and Office Depot had huge critical mass. If you don't ramp up a start-up as fast as competitors do, then it loses much of its value," says Westerfield. So WORKplace sold its California stores—we turned down the chance to buy them—and used the proceeds to expand its inventory and add six stores to the four it already had established in the Tampa Bay region.

Though WORKplace was still a speck compared with Office Depot, it began to develop a terrific business in Florida. It was the first clone to expand heavily into consumer electronics. As WORKplace sales began to grow impressively, Office Depot took notice. It had no stores in the Tampa area and decided to make an offer to buy the upstart company. Westerfield and the board were insulted by the low buyout price that Office Depot proposed, according to industry sources. But Westerfield asked to meet David Fuente, Office Depot's CEO, to discuss the offer.

They met at the National Office Products Association show at McCormick Place in Chicago. After finding a private booth, Westerfield sat down with Fuente and Steve Dougherty, Office Depot's president. Westerfield's point to the two executives was simple: WORKplace's investors would consider selling the company, but it was worth much more. As he explained how WORKplace's stores were progressing, Fuente listened closely and Dougherty tensely chain-smoked cigarettes. Then, say sources familiar with the incident, Dougherty jumped to his feet. "If you think we're going to allow you to make profits in these Florida stores, you've got another thing coming!" A few minutes later, he left the room. Fuente looked embarrassed. Conversation became strained. Though they had decided on nothing, Westerfield reminded Fuente before they parted that he still had an interest in further discussions.

Two weeks later, Office Depot rolled out the cannons. It opened its first store in Tampa and unleashed an aggressive advertising campaign. Full-page newspaper ads screamed the news: Everything in Office Depot cost 15 percent less than in

WORKplace. Westerfield called Fuente and pointed out that the campaign's claims weren't true. Fuente seemed willing to look into the matter. But the ads continued. Office Depot next published its store catalog. Pictured on its cover were two hands ripping apart a WORKplace catalog. Office Depot's prices, the ad copy said, were 15 percent lower. Soon the picture became part of Office Depot's newspaper ads.

Westerfield protested to Fuente twice more. But the ads continued. Finally, he decided to take action. A small team of WORKplace managers bought fifty or sixty items from Office Depot's store. None of them sported prices below WORKplace's; in fact, they were more expensive. Westerfield took his beef to court, suing Office Depot for false advertising. Within ten days of the complaint being filed, Office Depot pulled its ads. Approximately six months later, a federal magistrate ruled in favor of WORKplace. The suit was finally settled out of court and a significant award was made to WORKplace, according to industry sources.

## TODD KRASNOW

Jack Bingleman grew up in Canadian business, was in real estate, and ended up being the CEO of the biggest home improvement chain in Canada. I can remember the early days of his starting Business Depot and Tom saying, "You can't let Office Depot do X, Y, and Z." And Jack would say, "Nobody would do that." And time after time, Jack, who is very savvy and had been around the block a number of times, was amazed. He was used to a very gentlemanly game of how things work.

I remember there was one site where we had a deal with Beaver Lumber, his old company, to take on the lease. Everything was set. He had had lots of dealings with his old company and the landlord, Conrad Black's Dominion stores. He had a letter of intent. Leases were being processed. And the next *(continued)*

But Office Depot wasn't the least bit cowed by WORKplace. While still in litigation over the advertising claims, Office Depot rented a billboard in front of WORKplace's store on U.S. 19 North. Having just moved the company's offices into that store, Westerfield saw the billboard being prepped for painting. A call to the billboard company clued him in to Office Depot's move, and he quickly devised a counteroffensive play. The billboard was finished at 7:00 one night. "Office Depot," the billboard announced in ten-foot-tall letters, "Biggest Selection, Better Service, Low Prices Guaranteed." But by 5:00 the next morning, Westerfield could look at the billboard with satisfaction. At his direction, a local landscaper had planted five mature Florida palm trees directly in front of the billboard. Office Depot's message was unreadable. Tampa's newspapers and radio and television stations loved the story—and invented their own jokes to go with it. Maybe Office Depot should "leaf" town, one reporter concluded.

know Office Depot had found a clause in the contract that said the owner could reclaim the site if the tenant found somebody to assign the lease to. So Office Depot went to the landlord and said, "Hey, here's a half a million bucks. We want the site." And they got it. The fact that somebody like Jack, who had a very big position in a big company, was taken aback by their aggressiveness says just how aggressive the industry is.

In the end, Bingleman did get $50,000 from Dominion stores for the trouble.

The stakes in Jack Bingleman's battle against Office Depot in Canada were even higher: his company's very identity in the minds of customers. When Bingleman launched his company, the Staples board was confident enough of its prospects to become investors, but they did not want to put the Staples name on a business that they did not control. So Bingleman came up with a list of possible names and settled on Business Depot. Immediately, Bingleman began the tedious process of registering the name for trademark status. The protocol, which can take years to finish, involved having the Canadian government publish the name, which it did, and waiting for a period of time during which objections to the name can be filed by anyone who chooses to do so.

Not long after Business Depot began opening stores in 1991, Office Depot acquired the Great Canadian Office Supply Warehouse, a retail chain. For a few months, the Florida company operated the chain under its original name. Then it began to change the store names to Office Depot. It was an extraordinarily threatening strategy. Office Depot sounded confusingly similar to Business Depot. "By the time they entered our territory, we had brought a lot of equity into the business. And we had to some degree become famous by having great selection and bringing prices down. So we didn't want someone else to come in and take advantage with look-alike merchandise and look-alike stores," explains Bingleman.

---

### COPY PAPER AND COFFEE FILTERS

One of my great strengths is that I have a good marketing mind. Even better, I can assess opportunities and devise ways to take advantage of them. How do I do that? It's simple: I put myself in the customer's shoes. It's called defining the market.

We started Staples as a stationery and office-supply store. Others sold business machines. There were hundreds of business machine dealers. And you could buy janitorial supplies at janitorial supply houses anywhere in town. For your office coffee, you could contract with a *(continued)*

But the real menace did not appear until early 1992 when Office Depot challenged Bingleman's right to use the Business Depot name. Losing the name would mean losing relationships with customers—in short, everything that matters in a retail business.

There were two pieces to the name issue. The first was Office Depot's challenge to the trademark. The only way to fight that was through the courts, which Bingleman began to do immediately. The second part involved common-law usage of names. When Office Depot began to enter the province of Ontario, where many of Business Depot's stores were located, Bingleman asked a judge to rule on whether the company could use the Depot name.

He had ample evidence supporting his case. The judge granted Business Depot an injunction against Office Depot. The Florida company could not use its name in eastern Canada. Because it had already begun to erect Office Depot signs over some stores, the company hurriedly covered the word Depot with tarps. "We started calling them 'Office Tarp,'" remembers advertising vice president Phyllis Wasserman. The trademark legal battle is still continuing in 1996, but the injunction was a critical victory for Staples.

server or you could buy your own from a local supermarket. People sometimes wonder why Staples, which is best known for selling things like paper and pens, would also offer garbage bags and coffee filters. The answer is simple: We start with our customers and ask what they consume. Obviously there are a lot of things that customers consume—everything from ice cream to memory chips—and you can't do it all. But to the extent that you can, why not define your offerings that way? We did.

REAL-LIFE LESSONS

*Pick your battles.*

Aggressiveness for its own sake is wasted energy. But fighting a threat that truly matters is paramount. Don't let a competitor's size prevent you from responding. Tiny WORKplace prevailed by pursuing legal redress. But a lawsuit isn't your only option. Westerfield's landscape caper not only turned the tables on Office Depot, it won WORKplace invaluable publicity.

# CHAPTER 8

# THE PRICE OF SUCCESS: GLORY AND INFAMY

For most entrepreneurs, taking their company public is the Holy Grail. An initial public offering, or IPO, betokens acceptance by the financial community and credibility among corporate peers. It turns company founders into multimillionaires. But in my case, the main reason to go public in the spring of 1989 was to maximize shareholders' value. I also understood the great trick to raising capital: It's better to get funding when your company is hot than to wait until you need it.

There were lots of other options. I had regularly fielded offers from would-be financiers and buyers, almost from the company's inception. But the office-supplies industry was heating up on Wall Street. A robust stock market was warmly embracing one new public company after another. Investment bankers had been making regular pilgrimages to Staples' headquarters, clamoring to be allowed to underwrite the company's IPO. Both Office Depot and Office Club now traded on the stock exchanges. Investors were so excited about the sector that one company, HQ Office Supplies Warehouse, successfully sold its shares to the public without having generated a drop of revenue. And Staples, the company that had invented the industry, had just logged its first quarter of profits. It was time.

I was as rigorously analytical in choosing my investment bankers as I had been in picking venture capital partners. I was determined to use our IPO as a springboard for further increasing Staples' value and growth prospects. And I refused to take chances with a firm that could not deliver multiple benefits. "You can get screwed really badly when you go public," says Dave Lubrano. "The tendency is to go talk to one or two investment bankers and then be at their mercy."

I began my research by grilling investment banks' customers. Who better to assess how investment banks executed initial public offerings than the folks who bought the stock of these just-public companies? I asked money management firms such as State Street Research, Fidelity, and Kemper to rate the investment banks' credibility and research analysts.

The quality of a firm's research analysts was paramount. Wall Street analysts, who recommend stocks to large institutional investors, could have a huge impact on how well Staples stock performed. The best analysts' confidence in a company could keep its stock trading at high levels for years. Moreover,

I knew that if an analyst's firm underwrote our IPO, the analyst was obliged to cover and report on the company. Ultimately I wanted the bank to tell the Staples story to investors, and that's mainly a function of the analysts they have.

After polling investment banks' customers, I turned to the firms themselves. "Most companies [about to go public] don't do their homework when it comes to investment bankers," says Bo Cheadle, the Montgomery Securities analyst who began visiting Staples in 1988. John Berg, a managing director at Montgomery, remembers receiving four pages of questions about Montgomery's initial public offerings experience. Among them: How would the firm value Staples? How have the firm's IPOs performed? What are the firm's biggest accounts? Which of the firm's research analysts cover retailing? What are their records? And on and on they went. It took Montgomery six days to collect the answers. But that was only the beginning of what I wanted to know. "There were two or three requests for additional information, culminating in a formal presentation to Staples," says Berg. "This was hands-down the most intensive selection process of investment bankers known to mankind."

By late 1988, I had chosen a team of bankers. William Blair, a Chicago firm that scored extremely well in my rating system, would co-manage the deal with Montgomery. While the San Francisco firm hadn't ranked quite as high as Blair, Montgomery held a small company conference every year that was one of the two best in the country. Staples would be well served by becoming a showpiece on that stage. We awarded the lead management position to Goldman Sachs, the Tiffany's of investment banking.

Then the fun began. Going public is the financial and legal equivalent of stringing up your underwear for everyone to examine. And the examination is endless. "It's an immense amount of work. I can never describe how difficult it was while also trying to run and nurture the business," says Bob Leombruno. To negotiate the terms of the deal, we huddled with the bankers and lawyers in our rundown California Street headquarters. "This building was decrepit, with little heat. We used to joke about the rats joining us at our meetings. We couldn't complain though, because Staples needed to have the lowest cost structure in the industry," says Berg.

The jokes dried up during the next step: preparing the offering prospectus, a document describing the company, which is filed with the Securities and Exchange Commission and given to potential investors. Drafting sessions, as they are called, are among the most tedious time-wasters an executive ever encounters. Accountants, investment bankers, and lawyers from the two firms crowded into the conference room of our law firm for 12- to 14-hour meetings. The sessions entailed hours of endless questioning by the lawyers and bankers who wanted reassurance that they were not misrepresenting the tiniest detail to investors. "How can we be sure that there won't be an eminent domain event on this site?" "Can you give me comfort that there's no risk of obsolescent inventory?" They just wasted hours of time, and we got sucked into it. At 10:00 one night, we sat, exhausted, around a littered conference table. Gary Balter, an investment banker from Goldman Sachs who was such an avid hockey fan that he scheduled drafting sessions around Boston Bruins hockey games, portentously asked to be left alone in the room with the Staples managers. His question concerned our landlords. He said, "Let me ask you a very difficult question. Our investigations show that one of your landlords is a convicted felon. Does that surprise you?" I said, "Not whatsoever. What surprises me is that there's only one."

Once the offering documents were filed with the Securities and Exchange Commission, we embarked on the most critical phase of going public: whetting investors' appetites for Staples stock. We went on a 17-day "road show," traveling around the world to present the company to potential investors. A normal road show has a hellish schedule, as bankers try to squeeze as much

## JOHN WILSON

You want the stock price to be high in an IPO because you want to maximize the proceeds to the company. But there are all kinds of other pricing pressures, too. Look at the "spread" you pay the investment banks, which comes out of the proceeds from the IPO. We gave the bankers a high spread of 7 percent because we wanted the bankers to feel good and have an incentive to make sure the deal is successful. This is particularly important over the long run because you want to come back to the market in the future. It's a fine balance that a CEO must strike. If you leave investors feeling happy, because the shares they bought at 19 are now trading at 25, they say, "Yeah. I'll buy some more in the next round."

exposure to as many investors as possible into each 24-hour period. Our road show was more brutal than most. John Wilson, our chief financial officer, called me the Energizer Bunny of finance. Investors had already heard that this was one IPO that should not be missed. "The presentations were absolutely packed," remembers Berg. "It was clearly what we all call a hot IPO."

The emotional pitch of these jam-packed days ranged from euphoric highs to oppressive lows. New York's classy Plaza Hotel was one of the last stops. I took the opportunity to make peace with Fred Adler, the venture capitalist who helped launch both Staples and its archrival Office Depot. I invited Adler to sit at the presenting table with the Staples executives, and in my speech I paid homage to Adler's sponsorship. He glowed.

During one leg of the U.S. journey, Bob Spellman, Staples' senior vice president of finance at the time, and I missed a connection from Atlanta to Boston. Opting to get as close to home as possible, we caught a flight to Philadelphia instead, landing at 1:00 in the morning. There were no more flights to Boston and we were exhausted. But getting a hotel room for less than half a night's sleep would be frivolous. I curled up with my suitcase on a vinyl waiting room couch and conked out.

---

**IN MY OWN WORDS**

My mother-in-law had an M.B.A. from Wharton and was a very savvy investor. Now her son-in-law was taking his company public and she planned to buy 1,000 shares in it—a big investment. So she tells me she wants to attend one of the road show meetings. I'm worried that she might want to attend the really big one that everyone attends in New York at the Waldorf Astoria. I asked Goldman Sachs, "Are we going to make a stop in Philadelphia?" The bankers said no. I said that we should go. So after meeting T. Rowe Price in Baltimore, we get on a Metroliner to go to Philadelphia and have lunch at the Four Seasons Hotel. There were about 20 potential investors, venture capitalists, and investment bankers there—plus my mother-in-law.

All of the Staples executives had been thoroughly drilled on how to respond to questions. If somebody asks you about a competitor, you say nice things, no matter *(continued)*

---

Selling the Staples story abroad brought me some of my best—and worst—moments. Starting in London, Michael

Cohrs, a Goldman banker whom I had known at Harvard, put together a perfect day. The Staples team stayed at the elegant Savoy Hotel, and we met individually with investment giants, such as Mercury Warburg, throughout the morning and afternoon. The lunch presentation, to which the rest of the financial community was invited, was jammed.

Full of excitement and high hopes, we left for Switzerland at 6:00 the next morning. We met with a small group of potential investors at Goldman's Zurich office. Within minutes of the introductions, the Goldman banker in charge of selling Staples stock asked a question that shocked me. "How," he wondered, "was Sta-

how much you hate them. So one of the analysts from Delaware Management asks me how we compare ourselves with Office Depot. My answer was, "They're a great company. Their approach is a little different from ours. They come from the lumber industry. We're supermarket guys. We believe in something else." Toward the end of my answer I hear my mother-in-law's cane thumping on the floor. "He's LYING," she screamed out. "I've been to the stores with him. That store is a dump. D-U-M-P!" It was one of those incredible moments. I put my arm around the Goldman Sachs banker and said, "Aren't you glad she came to Philadelphia instead of New York?"

ples different from Price Club? And didn't it have the same business issues to wrestle with?" Price Club, of course, was a grocery and general merchandise chain—a completely different animal, in other words. The question might have been acceptable if it had come from an investor. But here it was, coming from the mouth of a professional who was supposed to know Staples inside and out to sell the stock. I went ballistic and started yelling and screaming at the Goldman banker. John Berg honestly thought I was about to give Goldman the boot.

Zurich had been a totally useless stop, but we were heart-ened when we returned to London, where orders for Staples stock continued to stream in, and boarded the Concorde. Arriving at JFK International Airport at 5:00 P.M., we lobbied USAir to board its 5:30 flight to Baltimore, instead of the 8:00 flight we had booked. While we were waiting, I returned a call from Bobby Haft, whose family owned and controlled Dart Drug. Haft told me he wanted to buy Staples. I wasn't inter-ested in selling. As I hung up, I fretfully calculated whether or not Haft could mount a takeover attempt. No, I decided. Back at the gate, we were given seats on the 5:30 flight.

A few hours earlier we had been jetting back from Europe on the Concorde. Now I found myself in the last row of a lit-tle turboprop with my knees jammed into the reclined seat in front of me. I thought my legs were going to fall off. Finally the plane landed. Exhausted, we searched for the limousine that was supposed to ferry us to our hotel. It wasn't there. It turned out that one of our own investment bankers had hijacked it. A taxi then, we thought. But it was Passover and most of the cabbies were on holiday. At last, after waking in London nearly 24 hours earlier, we found someone to take us to the hotel where we collapsed.

The grueling work paid off. In late April, the road show was successfully completed and market conditions were per-fect. In an ideal IPO, demand for the new stock far outstrips supply. "You want it to be four to ten times the actual number of shares available," says Wilson. The price of a share of stock should be set high so that as much money as possible is raised. But it can't be so high that the share price falls after the first day of trading. Investors' appetites for Staples shares were so keen that the investment bankers had already reset the price range once. Initially set to come at $13 to $15 per share, the share price was revised to $15 to $18 per share before the final documents were filed with the SEC. Now demand from institutional investors was eight to ten times the supply of stock. The bankers decided to nudge the price up once more, to $19 per share. When the first Staples shares began trading, I was in my office trying to get back to work. It was tough to do. As the stock began floating up, members of the executive team, whose shares in Staples were enriching them by the minute, kept popping into my office to report on the stock as it was bid up by enthusiastic investors. The stock surpassed $23 and closed at $22 ½, 18 percent above the offering price. We raised $61.7 million. "It was one of the fastest, most successful IPOs since the crash in 1987," says Wilson.

## REAL-LIFE LESSON

### *Don't stint on promotion for your IPO.*

We had a terrific story to tell, of course, but we also recognized that the stock price would benefit most by getting out there and telling the story rather than stinting on investment banker fees. You're far better off paying the investment bankers a decent fee and feeding their enthusiasm for the deal than trying to nickel-and-dime them. Justly or unjustly, an IPO's success has as much to do with showmanship and market buoyancy as with your company's true worth.

# Professional Naysayers Have Their Say

Though going public can make you rich, it can also subject you to slings and arrows whose sting is all the more painful because they are unwarranted. As befits a fast-growing company, Staples stock was quickly awarded a high price-to-earnings (P/E) multiple, meaning it usually traded at 40 to 50 times its annual earnings per share. Though a high P/E is a positive sign of investors' happy expectations, it also makes a stock especially sensitive to even the slightest whisper of bad news. Why? Its high-growth characteristics attract a breed of investors known as momentum investors, who buy stocks with rapidly accelerating earnings and sell them on the tiniest of disappointments over a company's prospects. "Our stock is one of the most volatile in the market. Any slight concerns are multiplied and magnified," says John Wilson.

We learned how dramatically such concerns could hurt Staples' standing in the financial community in the fall of 1990. In late September, David Childe, an analyst with San Francisco–based Robertson Stephens & Co. who had been covering the office superstore industry for just over a year, issued a three-page report cutting his earnings estimates for companies in the industry. Such revisions can trigger a sharp sell-off as investors rush to bail out of a stock. This one felt particularly damaging. First, it came as a complete surprise. Instead of alerting us to his change, as was customary, Childe simply faxed the report out to institutional investors. Second, the analyst recommended that investors not only sell the stock, but sell short—in other words, bet on the stock falling. Staples stock had already been under pressure, falling from $25.50 in July to $16.00 just before Childe's report. It fell another 15 percent in the days following Childe's assessment that we would be unable to crack the California market with profitable stores. All of this occurred while Childe was still publicly maintaining a "hold" rating on Staples stock.

Surprised and angry, Spellman and I called Childe. If he didn't have the courtesy to alert us to his change of opinion, we told him, we would not have much interest in keeping him abreast of company developments.

A chagrined Childe quickly followed up the tense phone conversation with an apologetic letter. He agreed to notify us of any pending estimate changes and promised to supply drafts of his research reports prior to publication. "Though we may differ at times, in no way would I ever intentionally undermine Staples' considerable achievements in the industry that you pioneered," he asserted in the letter.

The pattern of negative reports containing often-faulty reasoning continued for a month or two. Then Childe began faxing his early drafts, which Spellman or I corrected by faxed letter. A meeting with Childe and his boss, Michael Stark, in January had begun to ease the strain. But on February 19, 1991, Childe faxed a draft of a report in which he cut his earnings estimate for Staples' fiscal fourth quarter. Spellman didn't see the draft, which reached our offices at 8:00 P.M., until 7:30 A.M. on the 20th. He tried unsuccessfully to reach Childe twice only to discover that the report had been released at 1:40 in the afternoon. Once again, Childe had given us no chance to respond to his extrapolations. And once again, the analyst began issuing reports asserting that his estimates were based on company "guidance," when in fact we had provided none.

I decided on a new strategy. Not only would we cut off ongoing communication with Childe, we would no longer correct his drafts, even if he sent them. I wrote to Stark, pointing out Childe's errors and noting that clients of Robertson Stephens & Co. who followed Childe's advice might not be faring well.

The summer of 1991 passed. Childe continued to forecast weakening profit margins. By fall his dark outlook became more threatening. Childe again recommended selling Staples stock but, worse, had begun actively espousing his view in the media. In November, CNBC aired a story about Office Depot and Staples. It might as well have been called "Beauty and the Beast." According to the story, Office Depot was in a lovely position—essentially without any competitors invading its territory—while a big chunk of Staples stores were about to suffer an assault from OfficeMax. Childe was not only referenced in the story, he seemed to be the only source for it.

Being wrong didn't seem to alter Childe's stance. He'd first recommended selling Staples short when it was at $13 per share. But the stock had continued to rise. Now, in early 1992, it was trading at about $30. Its astronomical P/E—now nearly 70—as well as Childe's constant refrain had attracted a number of short-sellers.

Our strategy of ignoring Childe and the shorts to focus on our business seemed like the best course until the next time the story hit the press. I was in court on a personal matter when Dan Dorfman, a columnist for *USA Today*, called for me. When I returned the call, Dorfman repeated the shorts' assertions: OfficeMax and Office Depot would soon be making inroads into Staples' kingdom in the Northeast, driving margins down. I said, "Look, can I go off the record?" He said, "Sure." I said, "We're going to bury the shorts, and here's why. . . " The gist of my argument: OfficeMax would have more difficulty getting the real estate locations than they thought they would. And also, our plan to lower prices would likely lead to greater market share.

After our conversation, Dorfman's March 30th column was a shock. "Pros: Staples to get hammered. CEO rails against crit-ics." The story's first paragraph was even worse: "Repeatedly cursing and often speaking so fast I couldn't keep up with him, Tom Stemberg—43-year-old CEO of Staples, the country's second-largest chain of office-supply superstores—blasted his company's critics. 'They're so full of s***,' he says. 'I'm so [expletive] angry. It's outrageous what the [expletive] shorts are doing,'" wrote Dorfman. Childe was quoted saying, once again, that investors should sell Staples stock.

> ### ON GOING PUBLIC
>
> People sometimes ask me whether I was nervous on the day Staples went public. By the time you get to that stage, there's not much you can do about it. The deal is done at that point. A lot of people go down to Wall Street and ring the bell. That's not my style.

It was a vicious story. It made me look like a complete ass and buffoon. Our requests for a correction were ignored, but history has borne out my confidence. By the end of fiscal 1992, same-store sales were up 16 percent and Staples stock rose to $33.50. (By the end of fiscal 1995, the stock had risen 124 percent above the 1992 level, adjusted for stock splits.) Childe eventually left Robertson Stephens & Co. And Dorf-man, who left *USA Today* to become a columnist at *Money*, resigned from the magazine in 1996 because he refused to divulge his sources for other stories to *Money*'s editors.

REAL-LIFE LESSON

*Don't try to control what's out of your control.*

You can—and should—build working relationships with analysts and reporters. But if they cannot be reasoned with—or flout the agreements you made with them—they are not worth your time. When they cross the line, you've just got to let them know it.

## Under Fire

Not all of the public controversy that Staples engendered revolved around its stock price. In the fall of 1994, the company inadvertently became the center of a storm that erupted over Mitt Romney's campaign against Edward Kennedy for a U.S. Senate seat. Romney was an accomplished businessman, not a politician. As head of Bain Capital, he had backed our crucial first round of private financing and by 1994 had invested $2.3 million in the company. In 1990, he temporarily returned to Bain & Co., the debt-ridden, floundering consulting firm for which he had once worked, to implement a successful turnaround. And though he is the son of George Romney, a three-term Republican governor of Michigan during the 1960s, his political heritage counted for nothing in Massachusetts, where the Kennedy name had been winning Senate seats on the Democratic ticket for 32 years.

It was a tough fight. The top three issues were crime, welfare, and jobs. With the election three months away, Romney began airing radio ads in which he claimed that he would be more effective at creating jobs than Kennedy. He had no record to support such a declaration in the political arena, of course, but ample evidence from his business career. The fast-growing companies in which Bain Capital had invested had added between 10,000 and 17,000 jobs. Staples, one of the premier success stories in Bain's portfolio of companies, was a key job generator, having zoomed from zero to 10,000 employees in eight years. And I was an outspoken supporter of Romney, acting as co-chair of the campaign finance committee and willingly granting interviews to the Boston reporters who called.

In the Kennedy campaign offices, Romney's remark about job creation smarted. The Democratic strategists soon revealed how they would counterattack. "In politics you look for anything to hit your opponent with," says Romney. "They looked at all eighty companies in which Bain Capital had invested and tried to find the most damaging thing they could." On September 15, Romney held a 20-minute press conference in front of our first store in Brighton. With him were the CEOs of some of the companies he had funded, including Judy George, founder of Domain, a furniture and accessories chain, and me. We described how crucial Romney's support had been to our companies' success. A *Boston Globe* reporter lobbed an unexpected question at me: Did Staples offer its employees health insurance? Like most retailers, we offered health-care benefits to full-time employees but not to part-timers, I told the reporter. When Romney took the microphone, he stressed the economic benefits of job creation. "I appreciate Ted Kennedy's years of service, but I don't think he has a clue to how to create jobs," he said. The

*Globe* reporter later called Rick Gureghian, Kennedy's campaign spokesman, for a response to Romney's comment. According to an item in the next morning's *Globe*, Gureghian said, "Mitt Romney is pocketing millions of dollars creating service-industry, $4.50-an-hour, part-time jobs that do not pay health insurance. And Mitt Romney thinks that's something to brag about?"

> ### SALE DAY
>
> Sale day is a real catch-22. If the stock trades lousy, you come away depressed and unhappy. If the stock trades great, you look around to see if there's anything left on the table, and psychologically that's not a great thing to do. After the IPO, I knew that Staples would probably continue as usual. I have to admit, though, that I knew I would be really mad if the stock price at the initial offering fell below our expectations.

I was infuriated. But I got even hotter as I sat reading the newspaper in the kitchen of my country house in Marion, Massachusetts, the following morning. Saturday's paper contained a story describing Kennedy's plan to run a series of get-tough television ads that would expose the "real" Mitt Romney. The theme was that these are bad jobs Romney helped create. It sounded like they would go on the air making false accusations. I called around town and soon discovered that the advertisements did involve Staples.

I started a two-pronged campaign to straighten out the health benefits issue. The first step was to try to informally negotiate with Michael Kennedy, Senator Kennedy's campaign manager. The second step was to formally complain. On the morning of September 19, I faxed a letter objecting to Gureghian's comment in the *Globe* to Kennedy's Washington, D.C., office. "These statements are flagrantly incorrect," I wrote. Moreover, they could damage the company's reputation and that of the 2,000 Staples employees who were

Massachusetts residents. "You do represent them and their families, do you not?" I wrote. There was dead silence from the Kennedy camp all day long.

Finally, at 10:00 P.M., a two-page letter from Michael Kennedy popped out of the fax machine in my home. In it he asked eleven questions about Staples' wage and health benefits policies. "What contribution to coverage does Staples make to the cost of coverage for employees qualifying for coverage? Does this contribution vary among employees? If so, please describe the differences among salaried and hourly employees, low- and high-paid employees, more- and less-senior employees, etc." The clincher was that Kennedy wanted answers to these detailed questions by noon the next day. "If I do not hear from you by noon on Tuesday, September 20, 1994, I will assume that most of your employees do not receive health benefits through your company, and you can expect continued public discussion of these issues."

I decided to cut to the chase. Instead of filling out the questionnaire that Kennedy had devised, I wrote a short letter containing two facts: Entry-level wages at Staples exceeded $4.50 an hour and more than 50 percent of our employees received health benefits paid by the company. Though the Kennedy crew never publicly corrected their statements, they did refrain from using the Staples name in their television ads.

Such facts hardly seemed to matter amidst the avalanche of aggressive advertising mounted by Kennedy's well-oiled campaign machine. Romney lost. "My campaign was affected by the fact that I'm in business and that my opponents' campaign very skillfully took small features of our various investments and tried to make them into major events," concludes Romney.

## REAL-LIFE LESSON

*Standing up for who you believe in isn't always pleasant.*

One of the perks of success is that you and your company become better known and more influential. But a high profile makes you vulnerable as well as powerful. Any time you take a stand, you take the chance that you're going to expose yourself to negative press. It's part of the package, so don't be shocked when it happens.

# CHAPTER 9

# MISTAKES:
# REAL AND IMAGINED

The cliché is that hindsight vision is 20/20. But even hindsight is a matter of perspective. Today you may think a five-year-old decision was a mistake. In another five years you may not. What we see as blunders look that way only because our view of the world has changed. We made our share of errors, all for what seemed like good reasons at the time. None was fatal, and some were actually helpful. Examine them together, though, and you see a road map of a gradually maturing business philosophy. Here are the missteps and what we learned as a result of them.

SNARING OFFICE DEPOT Some might argue that the most colossal error we made was not buying Office Depot, the Florida clone that grew faster and became bigger than Staples. Interestingly, we might not have had the chance to buy the company if not for a previous "mistake." The error? Allowing Fred Adler, one of our initial venture capitalists, to indirectly back a rival office-supplies chain—which turned out to be Office Depot—after he had invested in Staples. Within a year of Adler's "treasonous" act, his advisor, Joe Pagano, called me with some news: Pat Sher, Office Depot's founder, was dying of leukemia. The board was considering two options. No. 1: Get another infusion of venture capital and bring in new management. Or No. 2, the action Pagano favored: Merge Office Depot with Staples.

> ## RAZING EXPECTATIONS IN QUARTERLY REPORTS
>
> The current financial-reporting system leaves a lot to be desired. Take the quarterly earnings report, for example. It's a terrible way to manage a business. The notion that every quarter you have to account to the investing public for every dollar sometimes forces you into a bind. If you miss projections by 1 percent, the company's value gets whacked. You are forced to make decisions for the near term to manage this quarter-to-quarter earnings flow rather than doing what is right for the long term.

It was a great opportunity. We could leapfrog ahead of the sea of clones that had arisen in our wake and do so with the second-strongest company in the fledgling industry. But I felt torn. Office Depot operated in a totally different part of the country, picked its store sites with a completely divergent strategy, and—most worrisome—functioned with a "shoot 'em up cowboy" culture. After discussing the acquisition with

Bob Leombruno, Paul Korian, and Myra Hart, I decided to go for it. At best, I'd get the company. At worst, my interest would drive up the value of Office Depot, which would benefit Joe Pagano and, indirectly, Fred Adler. I told Adler I was willing to offer $12 million for the Florida company.

But the venture capitalists who controlled the company rejected the offer. Rather than selling out, they wanted a bigger score. They wanted to go public as soon as possible. I could have offered more money, but I was nervous about managing Staples and Office Depot. In the final analysis, I was chicken. In those days they were a bunch of cowboys, and they didn't want to sell to us. It would have been a difficult merger.

## REAL-LIFE LESSON

### Be bold!

The merger undoubtedly would have been difficult, but would the merged company have failed? Probably not. We would have learned how to operate in nonurban settings much earlier than we did, and Office Depot's managers would have learned how to study and refine their successes much sooner.

CAPTURING OFFICE CLUB While I let Office Depot slip away with few regrets, another missed chance filled me with anxiety for weeks. Once again, it involved Office Depot, as well as another rival, Office Club. In the fall of 1990, I ran into Office Club CEO Mark Begelman at Morton's Restaurant in Chicago, where we both were attending the National Office Products Association convention. Begelman had spurned me ever since Staples entered the California market, which was Office Club's home turf. I asked Begelman about the rumors that Office Club was putting itself up for sale. Begelman confirmed them. His board had decided to sell the company, he said. I had always had a great deal of respect for Begelman, and I took the opportunity to apologize for the rupture in our friendship. Begelman seemed to accept it. Then I asked if we could talk about Staples acquiring Office Club. We agreed to meet in Baltimore, Maryland, the following week, when we both would be attending a conference sponsored by Alex Brown, a Baltimore brokerage firm.

I was incredibly enthusiastic about buying Office Club. Combining our stores with Office Club's would give us an unassailable position in California. Though Begelman seemed to welcome the idea of being acquired by Staples at our Maryland meeting, he called me in Framingham a week later to suggest that the discussions stop. Office Club's board would assess their options after the first of the year, he reported. So it was a complete shock to hear Begelman's message when I checked my voice mail one morning just before Christmas. He said, "Tom, I don't want you to read this in the newspaper, but you'll read it on the wire today. Office Depot acquired us."

It was a devastating blow. We hadn't even been able to throw our hat in the ring and make a proper bid for the company. And now Office Depot, our biggest rival, had captured the prize. The acquisition would make Office Depot three times as large as Staples. It was terrible. I remember wondering if Staples would end up as just another also-ran among a crowd of office-supplies companies. I didn't let on to many people at the time, but it was one of the worst moments I've ever had in business.

On reflection, I understood why Office Depot was extraordinarily attractive to Begelman. The California executive could not only sell his company to the largest company in the industry, but because Office Depot had a vacant slot, he could become its president. There were other ties, as well. Begelman had lived in Florida, and his wife was from the state. Office Club's venture capitalists were friendly with Office Depot's backers. The combination had personal and professional appeal.

> ### You May Be More Than What You Say You Are
>
> In this country we have forced companies to be highly accountable for whatever they say. This is not all bad; indeed, there are a lot of virtues to it. But one of the negative effects of this vigilance is that if orders don't match up, the analysts question the estimates and investors scurry away in fear. The SEC has passed rules enabling a company to make forward-looking, optimistic projections from a "safe harbor" without the threat of a lawsuit. At the moment, this ruling is still quite new and needs to be thoroughly tested and before it can be perfected.

Our response: Aggression. We quickly purchased ten California stores from HQ and stepped up the pace of store openings in Los Angeles. While the newly combined companies were in disarray, we focused like a laser beam on the California market. We were the first in the industry to mount a dynamic advertising and promotional campaign—and it paid off. Within two years we had established a six-store edge, and Staples was by far the most recognized office-supplies store name in Los Angeles. It wasn't revenge exactly—but it was just as sweet.

---

### REAL-LIFE LESSON

*How you recover is more important than the mistakes you make.*

Stunned as I was by Office Depot's new strength, I was galvanized, too. I looked for the shred of opportunity in the bad news and found it: We knew that Office Depot would have to reconcile two diverse concepts and real estate strategies. While they sorted it out, we could blow past them in Los Angeles.

---

SMALL-TOWN OPPORTUNITIES  In business, as in life, your outlook is irrevocably shaped by your origins. Because we started doing business in the Northeast, where the costs of doing business were extraordinarily high, we devised a strategy that would give us an advantage there: Establish superstores that were smaller than most, save on rent and operating costs, cluster them in densely populated areas to justify paying for expensive advertisements, and stock the stores from a distribution center. Born of necessity, this is the strategy that would not only allow us to make a lot of money but bar competitors from our turf.

It worked well, but we paid a price for the strategy's success: We couldn't see the potential in markets that didn't look like our home turf. Though Office Depot was planting stores willy-nilly, in towns with populations of just 75,000, we couldn't see how we could make money in small towns. The numbers didn't work. We assumed that the trading area was 10 or 15 minutes and that our market share would be the same as it is in large cities. So for year after year, we focused on New York, Boston, and Los Angeles, where we knew the formula would work.

Then, in August of 1991, we opened a store in Portland, Maine. With a population of 200,000, the town was smaller than most of our markets. But within months the store began doing extremely well. Customers were willing to drive much farther to get to the store, and because there was less competition, our share of the local market grew to be much higher than in denser urban areas. Joe Vassalluzzo and John Wilson both believed that operating costs would be much lower in small towns than in cities and urged me to experiment. So in 1992 and 1993 we opened Staples stores in places like Lancaster, Pennsylvania, and Victorville, California.

To our astonishment, the stores were total winners. We had not been able to make the numbers work because our most basic assumptions about a store's business were wrong when applied to a small town. Because small-town stores draw customers from farther away, sales are almost as high as for big-city stores. Yet rent is half as much, merchandise shrinkage is half, and advertising costs are a fraction of what they would be in more populous areas. Not going into small towns sooner was the dumbest thing we ever did. We were the last ones to move into them.

SELLING IN NEW WAYS  Because they have to work so hard
at bringing their vision to life, inventors of new business concepts can find it difficult to alter their idea. For us, the key
mental stumbling block lay in the term *low cost*. From its
inception, Staples' appeal was low prices. To offer those low
prices, we married a whole set of conditions. Costs had to be
low, so stores must be self-service and low on aesthetics. By
definition, we believed, Staples stores could not feature flocks
of attentive clerks and pricey, attractive finishing touches.

One of the first challenges to this fixed definition was the
customer who wanted delivery service. It was an obvious
unfilled need. Customers were buying office supplies in bulk,
as well as heavy items such as desks and file cabinets. They
clearly wanted—and asked for—delivery. But taking our low-
cost mission to heart, Staples' store managers found plenty of
reason to resist offering delivery. The question was: How
many customers really would use this service? "We didn't
want to add a lot of services because that would add cost to the
business, and we didn't want to add cost to all of our cus-

tomers to serve a few," explains Ron Sargent, president of the Contract and Commercial division.

The board argued vehemently against offering delivery and mail-order services. Their concern was that the delivery service could skew our business in such a way as to make it harder and harder to make a profit. If it costs you $60 to pick and pack merchandise for a delivery, but you charge only $15 for it, then you've given that customer a $45 subsidy. The more your business moves in that direction, the less money you're going to make. I was also worried that such a new service would dilute our efforts to grow our core business. But one by one, our competitors offered delivery and mail order. More importantly, our customers kept asking for the services.

So in 1988, we tested delivery and mail order in West Springfield, Massachusetts, and soon began rolling out the service throughout the chain. But it was a halfhearted effort. We did not go out of our way to let customers know that delivery was available. Our catalog was in black and white. And we penalized our best potential customers for using delivery service. The charge for delivery was 5 percent of

## THE MARKET IN SMALL TOWNS

Small towns are great. You can often find great people who are willing to work hard, and the wage scale is usually lower than that for the big cities. Publicity is practically free since people talk to one another over back fences and on street corners, and when someone finds a bargain, you can bet that the neighbors will know of it in short order. Like all retailers, Staples has had some theft that can be attributed to employees, but we find that it is much lower in the small towns than in the large cities.

the order price. So a customer with a $300 order paid $15. A big spender with a $2,000 order paid $100. "What we were doing was discouraging big orders. Simple logic would say you want to give customers an incentive to have a big order," says Sargent.

But it was two or three years before we decided to look harder and more objectively at this nagging issue. Sargent, who was put in charge of the tiny operation, hired Bain Consulting to investigate the mail-order delivery business. The findings: Customers who ordered from a catalog were not necessarily the same ones who shopped in the stores. "There's a lot of cross-shopping that goes on between retail and mail-order customers. But the mail-order customer tends to be a little bigger and a little more interested in service. The customers in stores are more often buying for home offices," says Sargent. In other words, instead of cannibalizing our basic business, the new services would enlarge our customer base. I have to admit, we could have done a better job understanding who our customer was.

## REAL-LIFE LESSON

*There's more than one way to serve your customers.*

When your strategy is working, nothing seems simpler than being very disciplined about executing it. That means not bending the rules. But sometimes a problem area, particularly one that is challenging your most basic assumptions, is pointing to a new way to provide customers what they want. If you can't see how to make that happen, advises Sargent, then get help: "We got outside help, and we got help from other parts of Staples that had the expertise."

# CHAPTER 10

# GETTING BIGGER: TURNING WEAKNESSES INTO STRENGTHS

Recognizing that there was a segment of the business—delivery and mail order—that we had treated like a stepchild was a significant insight. But deciding to mine the opportunity—and figuring out how to do it—were the really critical milestones. Our managers were forced to grapple with the question of whether to devote all their energies to expanding their core business or to pioneer a new one. And the consequences of this decision would turn out to be much larger than any other time they had faced that quandary. From 1991 (when we finally decided to set up the Contract and Commercial division as an independent unit) to 1995, the new business' sales grew from $30 million to $740 million. By the end of 1996, sales of the once-neglected business will probably exceed $1 billion—a level it took Staples itself nearly eight years to achieve.

One of the key events that led to our decision to legitimize the mail-order business occurred in 1991 in the competitive California market. By then Office Depot, HQ, and Staples all had matching prices for delivery of merchandise: $15 or 5 percent of the order amount—whichever was more. What was significantly different about our delivery businesses was that Office Depot generated a good chunk of its California sales this way, whereas we did relatively few. In mulling over the notion of changing to free delivery, Todd Krasnow realized that the modification could serve three important goals. First, if we offered free delivery, sales would rise considerably. Second, we would be the only one in the California market doing it—a competitive advantage that we could promote heavily. Finally, if and when Office Depot was forced to also offer free delivery, its margins would suffer, because it would be adding to the cost of business it was already doing. The strategy worked beautifully. And something unexpected happened. "We realized that as delivery volume went up, efficiency went up. Route density increased. Phone orders per order taker went up. So suddenly it was costing half as much—or less—to deliver. Instead of $20 per phone order, the cost of delivering fell to $9 per phone order," says Krasnow. As the economics changed, we realized this was a business opportunity worthy of attention.

But, odd as it sounds, plotting a course for the new business was especially difficult because of our large size. Trying to grow a new but complementary venture in an established company is like trying to cultivate a seedling in a garden plot jammed with mature shrubs—the big sturdy plants just naturally soak up most of the sunshine, water, and fertilizer. That was apparent from day one, when Ron Sargent was installed as the head of Staples Direct, as the mail-order business was named. Because mail order had always been a sideshow to the main event, many parts of the business were not thought through.

After taking charge of the unit, Sargent interviewed the hundred or so employees who operated the call center. Though each of these workers constituted the sum total of a Staples shopping experience, at least for customers who shopped only by phone, they did not feel like an important part of the company. They were paid different rates per hour, for no clear reason, and had no idea how to progress in the organization. Sargent provided an ear, brought order to the compensation structure, and designed a career path. He also had to cajole cooperation from employees who were used to focusing on store sales, not catalog sales. Sargent's new unit had no distribution system of its own, so it had to rely on the system that served the stores—but, of course, it didn't carry the same clout.

The most difficult obstacle to overcome, however, was the sense of competition that grew between the stores and Staples Direct. Because the store managers had always used the Staples catalog as a marketing tool, distributing it in the store and sending it to existing store customers, they were reluctant to give it up to the new unit. It felt like they were ceding control of their customers. Worse, they felt as though they got no credit when one of their customers placed a delivery order. "If a customer needs forty cases of copy paper, the easiest thing in the world for a store associate to do is to tell the customer to call the 800 number. Instead, you have situations where stores are saying, 'Well, I want to keep that sale in my store,'" says Sargent. Sharply divergent growth rates between the two areas reinforced the rivalry. Staples Direct's sales grew four times as fast as retail sales in 1995.

One by one, Sargent addressed these concerns. If a customer wanders into a store today and orders a desk to be delivered, the store gets credit for the sale, even though Staples Direct will pick, pack, and deliver it. What's more, a store's annual bonus is calculated, in part, by how well it has met its goals for generating delivery sales. The catalogs themselves are no longer filled with uninformative black-and-white line drawings. And though they are mailed to a vastly wider audience, existing store customers still receive them, too.

But the most significant change that stand-alone management brought to the mail-order and delivery business was a new lens through which to look at customers. Working with Bain, Staples' board member Row Moriarty, and me, Sargent analyzed who could be served by the new business. It was

---

**RON SARGENT**

When I got to Staples Direct, one of the first things I did was meet with every single employee in the call center, in groups of eight. It was interesting to hear the issues from their point of view. I mean, Tom said, "Here are the issues." And someone else said, "Here are the issues." It was incredible how different the priorities of the business are for those who actually interact with customers as compared with senior management. We thought that we just didn't have a great marketing strategy. That's what I had heard. What the employees were saying was, "There's no career path. I don't know what level I am. Some people are hired *(continued)* clear, from our earlier experience, that most of our delivery customers were companies with up to 50 workers. But what hadn't been clear was that we could also serve two other customer categories: medium-sized businesses (with 50 to 100 workers) and large ones (with more than 100). Looking out into the future, Sargent saw that if we built a separate system of distribution, merchandising, catalog operations, call centers, and other operations to support the delivery business, we could leverage off it to support sales to any size business—not just the smallish ones we had already hooked. So while the three segments would each have separate sales forces, the guts of their operations would be identical.

at $7 an hour and some people are hired at $8 an hour, and I've been here six months longer and I'm being paid $7 an hour." It was basic employee-relations issues. How could we expect them to up-sell and be nice to customers if they were so unhappy with their own jobs? Once you get that fixed, then you can say, "Okay, now, we've taken care of you. How do we take care of customers better?" It's not enough to have a great strategy; you need to address the people and the process of your business, too.

Figuring out this strategy up front allowed us to charge after our objectives in a much more focused and efficient way than simply letting the opportunity evolve. Because he was starting from scratch in trying to serve larger customers, Sargent embraced a growth-by-acquisition strategy. We had already dabbled with this by buying part of Eastman Stationers, a large contract stationer, in 1993. Though we acquired 16 percent of Eastman at a good price, our co-owners wanted to resell the company quickly—and at a much higher price. The equity value went from about $20 million to $80 million in three months. In the end, Eastman's business was not strong enough to justify buying the rest of it at that price, I believed, so we passed. Eastman was sold to Office Depot instead.

Within two years, however, we snapped up five regional stationers, and in February 1994 purchased National Office Supply, a contract stationer selling to Fortune 500 companies. Sargent's job quickly contained two contradictory imperatives: Spur a fast-growing business while simultaneously consolidating and streamlining the acquired companies. Puzzling out the steps was so painful and complex that Sargent's Monday morning meeting with his eleven key managers came to be dubbed "Partners In Hell."

"You know that you're planning to have one group that's going to buy product for our whole unit, and that group is going to be here, in Westborough, Massachusetts. But you can't have that buying group until, one, you move the right staff into Westborough, and two, we have a product line that's consistent throughout all of the acquired companies and our existing business. And we need to have computer and accounting systems that will support this consistent product line everywhere. It's kind of like a Rubik's cube," explains Sargent. "A year from now it's going to be a well-oiled machine, but we've got 12 months before we can say it's all integrated." Sargent has already made headway in reengineering the cost structure of the traditional contract stationer's business—with plans to extract 10 percentage points over next few years.

The fruits of this complex growth strategy are already apparent. By retaining the former owners of many of the acquired businesses, we have learned how to serve the Fortune 500 market faster than we otherwise would have—while holding onto key customers that we inherited through the acquisi-tions. "The companies that Staples acquired have been the cream of the crop. All of them have long-standing relation-ships with companies such as Xerox," says Henry Epstein, head of Staples Business Advantage, who sold his regional contract business to Staples in 1994.

In return, Staples has brought nationwide name-brand recognition and sorely needed capital to the business. We have invested in a new management information system, we have helped develop cutting-edge software that will allow cus-tomers to order products through their computers, and we can custom-tailor a special feature at a customer's request. After wooing Ford for six months, National Office Supply (now Staples National Advantage) won the contract to provide the automaker with office supplies in 1991. But it wasn't until NOS' team of five had flown to Dearborn, Michigan, for a planning session that they learned Ford wanted to be able to pay for its purchases with a credit card. By channeling pur-chases through a credit card, the auto company would be able to minimize its accounts payable expenses, because the credit card company would handle all the paperwork. It was perfect for Ford—but no one at Staples knew it was part of their plan. Instead of waffling over the special request, the Staples team hustled to create a system that would accept credit cards in just 90 days. They made the deadline and realized they had devised a new marketing tool. "Once we had the system, we were able to use it as a distinguishing feature from our com-petitors and implement it with customers like Pepsi Cola," says Evan Stern, the former president of National Office Supply who now heads Staples National Advantage.

*From tiny pockets of neglect, mighty businesses can grow.*

The disadvantage of launching a new enterprise in the middle of a fast-growing, profitable business is that it gets no respect. The advantage, though, is that once that new enterprise finds sponsorship, it can aim very high because it has the resources it needs. Don't let an afterthought to your main business be ignored for too long without thoroughly analyzing its potential.

## Shedding Skins: Make Way for the New

The challenges of growing Staples from a $3 billion company to a $10 billion company, which we plan to do by the turn of the century, are many. But one of the most important is symbolized by a vigorous, lengthy debate over an apparently simple matter: Should Staples stores feature concrete or tile floors? It sounds laughable. But it was, in fact, a pivotal issue. Because it showed that we couldn't grow in crucial ways until the organization was willing to shed old beliefs, old habits, and old paradigms. Making way for the new meant tossing out outgrown or outmoded notions.

But that is extremely tough to do. Concrete floors signified a whole set of associations. Warehouse stores have concrete floors because they are inexpensive to install and maintain. When I started Staples, I was emulating warehouse stores, with their low prices, so I opted for concrete floors. Silly as it sounds, concrete floors seemed as much a part of Staples' success as low prices because they were all wrapped

up in the original set of beliefs that created the office-supplies superstore concept.

But when Jack Bingleman joined Staples in 1994, after the company acquired the rest of his Canadian store chain, he brought a new set of beliefs: Low prices could coexist with a brighter, more aesthetically appealing store. "I felt that the stores, from the standpoint of Staples' customers, had become dull and unexciting. I felt that customers deserved a much more exciting and customer-friendly shopping experience," says Bingleman.

His proposal was dramatic: Redesign new stores to be larger and undertake a massive remodeling of the old stores. It was going to be incredibly expensive. And, in some ways, it seemed a frivolous expenditure when we were still building new stores at a frantic

## JACK BINGLEMAN

For the longest time, Staples resisted the fact that consumers, not just small businesses, came to the stores. We always said that we wanted to have small-business people shop at our stores, which would have included somebody that runs a business from home. But there's no such thing as the average situation. A home business can be anything from a serious, paper-intensive operation to a real estate agent to a retired person working on investments. While we were born to look after people who were running a business, over time it became clear that we were just the perfect place for students and teachers and consumers and others to come to. And then, when we saw how people came to us for office supplies, it was a natural that they would come to us for business machines. It isn't very long before you realize that there are more consumer computer-and-software buyers than there are business buyers. The same with office furniture. You could have sat there and said that the business customer is the only one we're interested in. But we evolved.

pace. To change definition of a Staples store, Bingleman had to introduce a new standard of measure. We should not judge the stores on the basis of improvements already made but on the basis of what the customer saw. "How did they look when you walked in the front door? How easily could you move around the store? Were we really doing a great job of buying regular and promotional and new forward-thinking, high-technology merchandise that really turned the customer on?" asked Bingleman.

His view prevailed. Remodeled stores are crisp and bright. Customers are no longer forced to move through the store the way they used to. They can buy more items that are new on the market... and the floors are tile. The decision has been validated by dollars and cents, too. Customers' response to renovated stores has been twice as good as the average retail remodeling gets.

---

### REAL-LIFE LESSON

#### *Growth hurts.*

It's scary to give up ideas that have made you a success. But you've probably outgrown some of them. Or the marketplace has rendered them obsolete. You and your organization can't move to a new level unless you jettison that baggage.

## Building an Organization: The Guts of a New Machine

After sawing off old, outmoded ideas, what do you replace them with? What's the bridge from a $3 billion company to a $10 billion giant? When we confronted that question late in 1994, we decided the answer had two components: a customer-oriented culture and the systems of a $10 billion company.

Marty Hanaka, a 20-year veteran of Sears, Roebuck, who joined the company as president and chief operating officer in 1994, believes that to get to the big leagues, every single employee's level of consciousness has to be raised. "The old days of putting together a 17,000-square-foot store with the grocery-store approach to basic assortments and letting a customer pick and choose, fill up a basket, and check out was probably fine at one time. To compete and win in the future we have to change from a pure operating company to one that is more customer service–oriented and sales-oriented," he asserts.

It's the kind of pronouncement that makes rank-and-file employees roll their eyes. Even at Staples, workers had heard it before. To make the transformation work, we began folding a customer-driven perspective into a multitude of efforts. First came the touchy-feely part: drafting a mission statement of the values we should all embrace and embody. Hanaka and I asked each operational area of the company to contribute one of their best people to form a task force that would have credibility within the organization. The group's final statement of values was CARE, an acronym for four areas of focus: customers, associates (Staples employees), real communications, and execution.

Rather than kick off the new mission with a three-by-five card in everyone's pay envelope, Hanaka and the task force, starting in 1995, have tried to integrate it throughout operations. It is built into the company's mystery shopping program. Customer compliments and complaints are categorized by function, so each area of the company knows how it is faring in meeting customers' needs. We formed a customer satisfaction group, which has been charged with accumulating data to correct problems at the root cause as well as anticipate trends.

Similarly, employees are measured and rewarded on the basis of how well they meet the principles espoused in the CARE mission statement. That standard, in fact, determines success more than job titles. "We're trying to create an organization and a workplace where we get the highest and best use of everybody. I don't mean this in a corny or superficial sense, but we want an aligned, functioning team where it doesn't matter what job or title you have . . . where what matters is winning as a company," says Hanaka. And if the company does win, in terms of prof-

---

## TODD KRASNOW

Opening and running one store is very different from having ten stores. When you go from one store to ten stores, you suddenly have to worry about systems: for hiring people, for getting the payroll done properly, for ordering your product and making sure all the stores are replenished properly. You can no longer do these things by hand. Then, when you get to be 100 stores, you need to worry about inventory control and shrink, issues that you didn't worry about before. The requirement for information systems changes radically as the business grows. It sure would be nice if somebody would periodically have said, "Okay, everybody. Time out! Now, we've got to change." But nobody knew enough to do that. You're just puzzling it all out as you go. You have an idea of what the company's various systems should eventually look like, but you don't know for sure.

its, then so do Staples employees. Most employees get a chance to own Staples stock through various plans.

In addition to transforming Staples' culture, the other large-scale change required before we can reach our $10 billion goal is to acquire the infrastructure—everything from technology to job slots—to support operations on such a scale. For years, my top managers and I could depend on simple proximity to stay abreast of all developments in the company. But by 1994, the company had grown much too large for that casual approach. In 1995, Hanaka called for the formation of a "point team" of seven key managers. "We're trying to create a method where there's regular communication, sharing of goals, alignment on policy issues and decisions. While we can disagree privately, we're going to be one cohesive, unified group to the organization," explains Hanaka.

Thinking on a different scale requires hiring in advance of truly needing a certain position. In finance, for example, CFO John Wilson has created three or four positions that simply did not exist before because one person could handle all the tasks. Having separate people handle tax planning, investor relations, treasury, and controller functions is crucial not only because those jobs will become more time-intensive as the company grows, but, if they are well-executed, they will have a huge impact on the bottom line. "When you're a $4 or $5 billion company, a 10–basis point improvement in this or that area becomes a very large number in extra profits," says Wilson.

One area in which anticipating fast growth has helped us achieve a competitive advantage: technology and information systems. Though analyzing and implementing new computer systems so frequently has been taxing, Staples workers get to use state-of-the-art systems. "Because they've had their systems so long, some of the old retailers can't really incorporate new developments. We're able to buy the best of the improvements and make the transition with limited expense," explains Wilson. The trick of getting increasing returns out of every small improvement is what will catapult not just Staples' information systems but the entire organization into the realm of the giants.

## REAL-LIFE LESSON

*Becoming a disciplined giant requires new disciplines.*

When your business is small, you don't need to think twice about your company's culture or philosophy. A common interest knits everyone together. But as your company grows, its sheer scale causes common interests to splinter. Managers can't single-handedly overcome that trend. Your principles and values need to be embedded in the company's systems to become consistent throughout.

# CHAPTER 11

# LESSONS LEARNED: A PERSONAL JOURNEY

Being an entrepreneur is a way of seeing into the future. For me, that meant envisioning a store that did not yet exist. As Staples grew, it meant enlarging the lens to encompass broader markets and varying strategies. Today it means foreseeing the engines of growth that will catapult Staples into the next century as a $10 billion juggernaut. Performing this forward thinking while solving everyday business problems is the first trick a company founder must learn—and one of the most useful at any stage of a company's growth. You have to live reality, but dream the dream.

But what does a company founder see when he looks backward? This book has mostly focused on real-life lessons that fledgling and established companies can draw from Staples' first, action-packed decade of life. But none of those truths could have emerged if I had not embarked on my own journey of learning and evolution. What became reality first started inside my head. Looking back, I recognize that my personal journey has taught me truths that have been even more essential than the corporate lessons. Here's what I learned.

## Never Underestimate the Potential of What You Are Doing

There is no shortage of forces that conspire to minimize your dream, to suggest that failure is the probable outcome. Like Darth Vader luring Luke Skywalker over to "the dark side," new competitors, experienced experts, even the status quo conspire against someone who is trying to do something new. Overcoming the siren call of failure is one reason never to sell your idea short.

The second reason is that, once you have begun, your idea will probably carry you much further than you expected. As Goethe said, "What you can do, or dream you can, begin it. Boldness has genius, power, and magic in it." Time and again, I underestimated how large and deep the U.S. market for office supplies would be. When I first started the company, my business plan estimated that Staples would be an $80 million company.

By 1990, I knew better—Staples itself had surpassed that sales level, and it had sizable competitors. The real limit, I thought at that point, was $1 billion. It was a much bigger number but not so big that I felt I could ignore its significance: Staples and its competitors would soon saturate the North American market, I thought. We had to act quickly to find business opportunities that would allow us to keep revenues growing rapidly. We were just very concerned that we would run out of room to grow. That is when we embarked on our two joint ventures in Europe.

Amazingly, the core appetite for our products and expertise just continued to grow. The ranks of the self-employed and at-home workers swelled. The nonbusiness consumer was increasingly attracted to Staples stores. And we finally discovered the unique rewards of serving small towns. Together these developments moved back the point at which we will simply be unable to find another corner in which to park a store. Here we are, six years after I worried about running out of room, and we are opening 120 stores a year. We are nowhere near the end of

## PERSONAL BACKGROUND

My father, Oscar, was Jewish and married my mother, Erika, a Catholic, in the early 1930s. Hitler was rising to power, and when the Nazis began "purifying" the workforce, my father got out of his native country. My mother, despite family objections, went with him. Eventually they settled in Newark, New Jersey, where I was born.

My father worked his way up in the restaurant business and made something of a success of it. But then he developed cancer and died from it. My mother decided to return to Europe to reclaim family property they had lost during the Holocaust. The authorities had announced that they would restore property to the survivors or their families. We went back to Vienna in the fall of 1967 and got back an apartment house that we had owned. I did a lot of growing up in Vienna.

growth in North American profitability. The new target: There will be close to 3,000 stores in North America before the market is saturated. As of the beginning of 1996, there were less than half that many.

## To See the Positive in a Sea of Bad News

If the defining characteristic of an entrepreneur is to see the future, my defining bias is to see opportunity in every setback. My entrepreneurial sense of optimism was best described by a joke that Bryant Gumbel, the "Today" show anchor, told me at a Friends of Harvard Basketball banquet. It's Christmas morning and two kids—one a pessimist, the other an optimist—open their presents. The pessimist gets a brand-new bike decked out with decals and accessories in the latest style. "It looks great," he says. "But it'll probably break soon." The second kid, an optimist, opens up a huge package, finds it filled with horse manure and jumps with glee, exclaiming, "There must be a pony in there somewhere!"

I have regularly called on my ability to wrestle good out of adversity. Two stores that lost money for Finast, my former employer, are now profitable

### ON HAVING DOUBTS

I always had doubts. I guess they never go away. Will the company grow ten more years? Will something screw up? The first quarter in which Staples made money—it was 1989—some of my doubts were relieved. But still . . .

I have seen a lot companies go through their ups and downs. It's amazing how many are just on the brink of success when something goes wrong. The statistics are sobering. The number of IPOs that do not have staying profitability hovers in the neighborhood of 40 or 50 percent. It's very high, and that will give any entrepreneur a lot of sleepless nights.

Staples stores. The Northeast, Staples' launching spot, was filled with extraordinary drawbacks: high labor, rental, and advertising costs. But my team and I turned those disadvantages into advantages by designing small superstores and building enough of them to keep out competitors and justify advertising. The unforeseen bonus to this approach: We are enjoying easy sailing in small towns like Keane, NH and Muskegon and Ocala.

When Henry Nasella, our chief operating officer, quit in 1993, I could have—and by some observers' reckoning,

> ## MANY ARE CALLED, BUT...
>
> To succeed as an entrepreneur, I think you have to have really tough skin. Whether you're just starting up or you're going public, there's so much crap that you have to put up with. It's easy to get yourself psyched out, and sometimes you do. You have to have tremendous mental stamina to deal with the beatings that you get. In the midst of the worst adversity, you have to keep your sights on your dream and sell your vision to whoever will help you realize it.

*should* have—wrung my hands. As the former president of Star Markets and Staples' day-to-day business manager, Nasella had a hands-on operator's credibility and had won the confidence of Wall Street investors. Without Nasella, analysts fretted, Staples might come unglued. But I did not see it that way. Instead I saw it as an opportunity to position the management that could take Staples to the next level and the next century.

## Lead by Example

This is probably the toughest rule to follow because it requires self-monitoring, self-control, and, most important, constantly reinventing yourself. Leading by example was pretty easy, in the beginning. When Staples started, there were so few employees and every one of us was so intensely involved in the same effort, it was natural to absorb similar values and priorities. But as the company grew, what was valued became murkier, more open to interpretation. And too often employees mistook what I like for what is best for the company. To paraphrase a comment from Bernie Marcus, founder and CEO of Home Depot: When word gets out that the chairman likes coffee, the next thing you know the staff buys Nicaragua.

I believe that the antidote to bureaucracy and politics is to resist the easy answers and search for a true picture of your business. When you get larger, more and more people tell you what you want to hear as opposed to the truth. I stay close to the guts of my operation by spending at least a day a week on the front lines, visiting stores, call centers, and distribution facilities. The more unfiltered truth I hear, the better. I also encourage risk taking by rewarding managers who spot problems or take on controversial issues. If you want people

---

## FUTURE DIRECTIONS FOR STAPLES

The rest of this century, our primary job will be to capture larger parts of the North American market with as many stores, office catalogs, and commercial businesses as we can develop. We will continue to focus on our customers and sell products at substantial savings. We still think that this market gives us huge opportunities. I don't exaggerate when I say that we can be close to a $10 billion company.

At the same time, we are looking to see what kind of legacy we want to leave, a growth vehicle that can sustain our expansion into the twenty-first century, beyond the growth that we have achieved so far. I believe the office-supply market will continue to grow into the next century. I think the company can still have a growth rate of 10 to 15 percent. Now that's an exciting and demanding future.

to try things, then you'd better create an atmosphere where you encourage it. Don't ream them after the fact if they try something gutsy and it doesn't work.

The most sophisticated way to lead is often the hardest for an entrepreneur, who is by definition a hands-on doer. It requires establishing the company's values and principles, and then stepping back to let others implement them. The man of action must become the man behind the curtain. It is a transition many entrepreneurs never pull off. But it is the most rewarding of all accomplishments.

What you really want to do is set in place principles and the broad outline of your objectives. But you don't want to worry about whether an innovation is your idea or somebody else's. One of my frustrations is when a member of my management team is

> ### ON TOM STEMBERG'S FUTURE
>
> I have a lot more years in me, but I'm not sure I have another five years in me to work at this pace! I would like to work at changing my role, becoming more of a mentor and creator. I think that is probably my greatest strength. It is assessing and figuring out how to take advantage of markets. I see my long-term role emerging around those activities as opposed to running a company that keeps on growing. We have a number of people who can do that far better than I can.

striving for recognition and insists on getting credit for something. They forget that it's much better to make it their people's idea. The most gratifying thing in the world is if your people do something exactly the way you hoped—arguably better than you would have done it yourself—without having to tell them to. That's the greatest feeling in the world.

# AFTERWORD

The next chapter of the Staples story opened September 4, 1996, as this book was going to press, with the announcement of the following.

> Staples, Inc., and Office Depot announced a definitive agreement to merge into a single company, Staples/Office Depot.* The new company expects to be able to provide even more customer savings and convenience as a result of the combined synergies and its more than 1,100 office superstore locations that will be renamed STAPLES, THE OFFICE DEPOT. Additionally, the combined mail-order and contract-stationer divisions should also be able to pass on improved savings as a result of this strategic combination.

As part of the new alliance, Thomas Stemberg, will serve as the new company's CEO, while Office Depot's Chairman and Chief Executive Officer, David Fuente, will serve as Chairman of the newly formed company. Martin Hanaka, President and Chief Operating Officer of Staples, Inc., will assume the same role in the new company.

Corporate headquarters for Staples/Office Depot will remain in Massachusetts. However, the company intends to maintain a significant and strategic presence in Delray Beach, Florida, where, among other functions, Office Depot's MIS department and Business Services division will continue to be located.

The Staples story continues to be a guide to forward thinking and successful management from genesis to innovation to the principles of large-scale, almost limitless growth.

---

*This merger is subject to customary closing conditions, including the approval of the stockholders of both companies and required regulatory approvals.

# INDEX

# Knowledge is Power

This maxim best describes why Knowledge Exchange (KEX) is dedicated to helping business professionals achieve excellence through the development of programs and products specifically designed to give them a competitive edge.

KEX's divisions include strategic consulting services; executive education, conferences and seminars; and multimedia, book, and online publishing.

The company's publishing division produces books that demystify the Internet, general business, management, and finance as well as audiobooks, videos, and CD-ROMs. KEX books and audiobooks are distributed throughout North America by Warner Books, Inc.

KEX was founded in 1989 by President and CEO Lorraine Spurge. Formerly a senior vice president at Drexel Burnham Lambert (1983-1989), she raised more than $200 billion for companies including MCI Communications, Turner Broadcasting, Viacom, Barnes & Noble, Mattel, and Tele-Communications, Inc.

KEX Chairman of the Board, Kenin M. Spivak, is also Cofounder, President, and Co–CEO of Archon Communications, Inc. He has served as President of the Island World Group; Executive Vice President and COO of MGM/UA Communications Co.; and Vice President of Merrill Lynch Investment Banking. He is also an attorney and a film producer.

For more information about the company or its products, visit the KEX Web site at http://www.kex.com or write to: Knowledge Exchange LLC, Publicity Dept., 1299 Ocean Ave. Suite 250, Santa Monica, CA 90401.

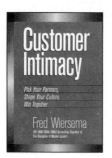

## The Accelerated Transition®

Fast Forward Through
Corporate Change

**MARK L. FELDMAN, Ph.D., and
MICHAEL F. SPRATT, Ph.D.**

An in-depth analysis of companies that have
gone through corporate change, with a concise
outline of proven steps to insure a fast, efficient and
successful transition.

**Hardcover/$22.95** (Can. $28.95)
ISBN 1-888232-28-5

Coming to bookstores in 1997

## Customer Intimacy

Pick Your Partners, Shape Your
Culture, Win Together

**FRED WIERSEMA**

Taking business far beyond the concept of good
*customer relations*, bestselling author Fred Wiersema
presents a new way of defining customer relations,
which has produced exceptional sales, profits and
customer satisfaction.

**Hardcover/$22.95** (Can. $27.95)
ISBN 1-888232-00-5
**Audiobook/$14.00** (Can. $17.00)
ISBN 1-888232-01-3
Read by the author

Available in bookstores now

## Changing Health Care

Creating Tomorrow's Winning
Health Enterprise Today

**KEN JENNINGS, Ph.D., KURT MILLER
and SHARYN MATERNA
of ANDERSEN CONSULTING**

An inside look at the health-care industry by a
team from the world's largest consulting firm,
laying out the essential strategies that companies
must follow to survive and thrive in the turbulent
health-care market of tomorrow.

**Hardcover/$24.95** (Can. $29.95)
ISBN 1-888232-18-8

Coming to bookstores in 1997

## Fad-Free Management

The Six Principles That Drive
Successful Companies and
Their Leaders

**RICHARD HAMERMESH**

A step-by-step program to implement the six
bedrock management principles that have a
proven track record in helping companies
achieve their goals.

**Hardcover/$24.95** (Can. $29.95)
ISBN 1-888232-20-X

Available in bookstores now

## Failure is Not An Option

A Profile of MCI

**LORRAINE SPURGE**

A case history that reads like a novel, this is the story of the tension, suspense, personalities and brilliant thinking that catapulted MCI from a start-up to a telecommunications powerhouse, forever altering the American business landscape.

**Hardcover/$22.95** (Can. $27.95)
ISBN 1-888232-08-0

Coming to bookstores in 1997

## Prescription for the Future

How the Technology Revolution Is Changing the Pulse of Global Health Care

**GWENDOLYN B. MOORE, DAVID A. REY and JOHN D. ROLLINS of ANDERSEN CONSULTING**

In a time of tremendous flux in the health-care industry, this book shows how those who can understand and harness changing technologies will be able to create the successful health-care organizations of the future.

**Hardcover/$24.95** (Can. $29.95)
ISBN 1-888232-10-2
**Audiobook/$12.00** (Can. $15.00)
ISBN 1-888232-11-0
Read by the authors

Available in bookstores now

## The Growth Strategy

How to Build a New Business into a Successful Enterprise

**PETER ENGEL**

A book that entrepreneurs have been waiting for, it shows businesses how to get beyond the start-up phase to become professionally managed businesses that will create true wealth for their owners.

**Hardcover/$22.95** (Can. $28.95)
ISBN 1-888232-30-7

Coming to bookstores in 1997

## The Pursuit of Prime

Maximize Your Company's Success with the Adizes Program

**ICHAK ADIZES, Ph.D.**

The renowned author shows companies how to successfully navigate the various growth stages of a business and reach *prime*—the stage at which they are most healthy and profitable.

**Hardcover/$24.95** (Can. $29.95)
ISBN 1-888232-22-6

Available in bookstores now

## Staples for Success

From Business Plan to Billion-Dollar
Business in Just a Decade

**THOMAS G. STEMBERG**

Written by the man who made Staples a reality, this
is the gripping story of how a simple idea was
turned into a new, multibillion dollar industry (with
key lessons for those who want to do the same).

**Hardcover/$22.95** (Can. $27.95)
ISBN 1-888232-24-2
**Audiobook/$12.00** (Can. $15.00)
ISBN 1-888232-25-0
Read by actor Campbell Scott

Available in bookstores now

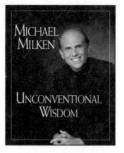

## Unconventional Wisdom

**MICHAEL MILKEN**

The man the *Wall Street Journal* called "the most
important financial thinker of the century" shares
his global vision, insight and ideas for the next
millennium, providing a guidepost for the next wave
of successful businesses.

**Hardcover/$25.00** (Can. $30.00)
ISBN 1-888232-12-9

Coming to bookstores in 1997

## The Tao of Coaching

Motivate Your Employees
to Become All-Star Managers

**MAX LANDSBERG**

A must-read for anyone who wants to get the
most out of their *human capital*, this book presents
a new way of approaching people management that
will allow your managers to use their time better
while motivating, developing and creating loyalty
among employees.

**Hardcover/$22.95** (Can. $28.95)
ISBN 1-888232-34-X

Coming to bookstores in 1997

## The World On Time

The 11 Management Principles That
Made FedEx an Overnight Sensation

**JAMES C. WETHERBE**

Learn how Federal Express became a phenomenal
success and discover the eleven innovative
management strategies they employed, which
have set the standard for the way businesses
manage time and information, handle logistics
and serve customers.

**Hardcover/$22.95** (Can. $27.95)
ISBN 1-888232-064
**Audiobook/$12.00** (Can. $15.00)
ISBN 1-888232-07-2
Read by the author

Available in bookstores now

## Business Encyclopedia: Master Reference

**KNOWLEDGE EXCHANGE EDITORIAL BOARD**

The ultimate business tool and the ultimate business gift, this illustrated reference book provides a wealth of information and advice on eight critical disciplines: accounting, economics, finance, marketing, management, operations, strategy and technology.

**Hardcover/$45.00** (Can. $54.00)
ISBN 1-888232-05-6

Available in bookstores now

## CyberDictionary

Your Guide to the Wired World

**EDITED AND INTRODUCED BY DAVID MORSE**

In clear, concise language, CyberDictionary makes sense of the wide-open frontier of cyberspace with information useful to the novice and the cyber-pro alike.

**Trade Paperback/$17.95** (Can. $21.95)
ISBN 1-888232-04-8

Available in bookstores now

## Business Encyclopedia: Management

**KNOWLEDGE EXCHANGE EDITORIAL BOARD**

Volume two of the Business Encyclopedia series, this book is an essential management tool providing in-depth information on hundreds of key management terms, techniques and practices—and practical advice on how to apply them to your business.

**Hardcover/$28.00** (Can. $34.95)
ISBN 1-888232-32-3

Coming to bookstores in 1997

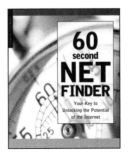

## 60-Second Net Finder

**AFFINITY COMMUNICATIONS AND KNOWLEDGE EXCHANGE EDITORIAL BOARD**

For people who want information from the Internet and want it now, this book shows where to find anything you want, in sixty seconds or less.

**Trade Paperback/$24.95** (Can. $29.95)
ISBN 1-888232-26-9

Coming to bookstores in 1997

# Free Tote with Purchase of Three Books!*

## I'd like to purchase the following books:

Number of copies

_____ **60-Second Net Finder**

_____ **Business Encyclopedia: Master Reference**

_____ **Customer Intimacy**
_____ *Also available as an audiobook*

_____ **CyberDictionary**

_____ **Fad-Free Management**

_____ **Prescription for the Future**
_____ *Also available as an audiobook*

_____ **Staples for Success**
_____ *Also available as an audiobook*

_____ **The Pursuit of Prime**

_____ **The World On Time**
_____ *Also available as an audiobook*

Name_____E-mail _____

Company_____Title_____

Address_____

City, State, Zip _____

Telephone _____Fax _____

Form of payment:

❑ Check (Make checks payable to **Knowledge Exchange, LLC**)      ❑ Credit card

Card # _____Exp. Date _____Card type _____

Cardholder's signature: _____

**Tell us more about yourself:**

| Occupation | Where do you buy business books? | How many business books do you buy a year? | Age Group |
|---|---|---|---|
| ❑ Professional | ❑ Bookstore | ❑ 0–3 | ❑ 18–28 |
| ❑ Technical | ❑ Mail Order | ❑ 4–10 | ❑ 29–34 |
| ❑ Clerical | ❑ Warehouse Store | ❑ 11–15 | ❑ 35–45 |
| ❑ Other | ❑ Other | ❑ 16 or more | ❑ 45–over |

**Knowledge Exchange** products are available wherever books are sold.
To order by fax, photocopy this page and fax to 714.261.6137
or call toll-free to order with your credit card

# 1.888.394.5996

*Offer expires Dec. 31, 1997 or while supplies last

Shipping and handling is $4.95 for the first book, $1 for each additional book, $2 additional for each *Business Encyclopedia*. Shipping is via Priority Mail. California residents please add 8.25% sales tax.